We Are Still Here

more from the author

Counselling Skills for Working with Shame
Christiane Sanderson
ISBN 978 1 84905 562 8
eISBN 978 1 78450 001 6

Counselling Skills for Working with Trauma
Healing From Child Sexual Abuse, Sexual Violence and Domestic Abuse
Christiane Sanderson
ISBN 978 1 84905 326 6
eISBN 978 0 85700 743 8

Introduction to Counselling Survivors of Interpersonal Trauma
Christiane Sanderson
ISBN 978 1 84310 962 4
eISBN 978 0 85700 213 6

Counselling Adult Survivors of Child Sexual Abuse
Third Edition
Christiane Sanderson
ISBN 978 1 84310 335 6
eISBN 978 1 84642 532 5

WE ARE STILL HERE

What Counsellors and Therapists Can Learn from the Lived Experiences of Child Sexual Abuse Survivors

Christiane Sanderson

Foreword by Fay Maxted OBE

Jessica Kingsley Publishers
London and Philadelphia

First published in Great Britain in 2024 by Jessica Kingsley Publishers
An imprint of John Murray Press

1

Content Warning: This book features accounts of child sexual abuse

A CIP catalogue record for this title is available from the
British Library and the Library of Congress

ISBN 978 1 78592 232 9
eISBN 978 1 78450 511 0

Printed and bound by CPI Group (UK) Ltd, Croydon, CR0 4YY

Jessica Kingsley Publishers' policy is to use papers that are natural, renewable
and recyclable products and made from wood grown in sustainable
forests. The logging and manufacturing processes are expected to conform
to the environmental regulations of the country of origin.

Jessica Kingsley Publishers
Carmelite House
50 Victoria Embankment
London EC4Y 0DZ

www.jkp.com

John Murray Press
Part of Hodder & Stoughton Limited
An Hachette UK Company

To all the survivors who contributed to this book, for their courage and strength, and to James and Max, for their abiding support.

Acknowledgements

I would like to thank all the survivors who contributed to this book, and those who expressed interest in telling their story. Your courage and strength in sharing your survival and journey to healing and recovery are inspirational. Without you there would be no book.

In addition, I would like to thank Linda Dominguez MBE, and all the counsellors and staff at One in Four. You do amazing work and truly understand the needs of survivors of child sexual abuse. This book would not have come to fruition without my editor Stephen Jones at Jessica Kingsley Publishers. His belief in the book and his consistent support in giving voice to survivors of child sexual abuse made the publication possible, despite Covid-19. Your support over many years has been unstinting and invaluable. My thanks also go to Emma Holak, for her thoughtful editorial guidance, and Pauli Roos.

I would also like to thank Dr Jo-Ann Cruywagen, Nicole Proia, Dr Emma Kay and Professor Anna Seymour, whose support spurred me on through the most difficult times. The support from my family is immeasurable and I thank you James, Max, Lucy and Natasha for your love and care.

Contents

Foreword

Years ago in the mid-1990s I volunteered to work on a helpline in the local rape and sexual abuse support centre. I'd returned to university as an adult student (social studies) and a fellow student saw something in me that made her think I would make a 'good volunteer' on the helpline for the local rape and sexual abuse support service. The training I attended was excellent. Groundbreaking even, and to this day still not replicated in the majority of health or even therapy qualifications. I remember vividly the session we had on the impact of rape and sexual abuse. The sense of horror and shame as I realised that I had or was still suffering from the majority of the trauma symptoms being highlighted by the trainer. Panic attacks, depression, suicidal thoughts, and on and on. But the setting was supportive and the trainers kind and caring. The training was cathartic for me and started a process of self-education, self-care and awareness-raising that continues to this day.

This book has the same power to affect, educate, inform and ultimately give hope for survivors and practitioners alike that there is a different life to be lived beyond trauma.

Once I started working in the sexual violence and sexual abuse voluntary sector I was captured by the need to support change and recovery for the survivors the agency worked with. Since those early days I have gone on to undertake training in transactional analysis, psychodynamic group work and counselling children and adolescents. As Chief Executive of The Survivors Trust, a national UK umbrella agency for specialist rape and sexual abuse support services, my work is now focused on advocating for effective support for victims and survivors of rape and sexual abuse in all its forms.

It's through my role as Chief Executive of The Survivors Trust that I first came to know of a groundbreaking psychologist, therapist and trainer that one of The Survivors Trust's founding Member Agencies, One in Four in London, had been fortunate enough to find to support their therapy, training and supervision. Christiane has a distinguished history of leading the way in writing about trauma and trauma-informed approaches and of challenging the taboos that surround sexual violence and abuse.

My work has brought home the dire lack of effective support and therapy services for victims and survivors. The specialist voluntary sector does an amazing job of trying to meet the ever-increasing demand for their services but continues to be under-resourced. Statutory services continue to have a poor track-record of recognising the needs of victims and survivors, let alone being able to offer the kind of support and therapy that is needed. Many of the survivors' narratives comment on having to seek private therapy before finding the kind of connection and relationship to therapy that makes the difference for them between merely existing or actually living a life that means something for them.

This remarkable book offers a platform where survivors' own words provide the narrative context of the book, without editing or interpretation. Truly allowing survivors to demonstrate their knowledge and understanding of their situations and experiences. I'm not a fan of the term 'experts by experience', particularly when applied to sexual violence and abuse since no-one wants to be an expert in these unwanted and unwarranted experiences. However, there is no denying that survivors are experts in how they have been impacted by sexual abuse and what might help them to cope and make the best of their lives.

Survivors' own words have tremendous power to convey so clearly the journey they have followed to reaching a moment in time when they can reflect back on the pain they have suffered and yet place themselves sufficiently apart from that pain to see what happened as a part of their experiences but not a part of them. That is, not the defining experience of their whole life. Reaching this understanding can be, and is often, an ongoing journey for so many. This is very clear from the narratives so bravely written and shared by the survivors and therapists.

The narratives bring together such a wide range of experiences, bringing to life the multiple factors that interact, intersect and amplify trauma for both survivors and therapists.

In reading the narratives I often recognised what was being portrayed. However, this book brought a totally new dimension to my own understanding of survivors' experiences.

As a survivor myself, so many times I found myself saying 'Yes, yes, that's just right', 'That's what it feels like'. I'm grateful for the honesty and generosity all of the contributors have shown in sharing so openly.

Underpinning the survivor and therapist narratives, Christiane brings a depth of knowledge and understanding of the ways sexual trauma in childhood impacts on relationships in multiple ways throughout someone's lifetime. Sexual abuse forces children to find ways of assimilating the conflicting fact of sexual violation with the need to preserve their belief in loving and caring adults. In a process of 'doublethink' children have to simultaneously accept two conflicting beliefs as the truth, often only achieving this by denying their own memories and experiences let alone their own sense of right and wrong in the world. Building trust with survivors is therefore fraught with complexity and is easily lost.

If you are looking for a book that will help you to understand what it means to be a survivor, you will find a treasury of experiences and wisdom. If you are a survivor looking to understand yourself more, you will find affirmation and validation in hearing from other survivors about the ways they have managed their own reactions and coping strategies and ultimately reached a point where the sexual abuse is one factor among many others that contributes to where they are now but importantly has lost the power to define them.

If you are a therapist looking for new insights into working with survivors, you will surely find every page is packed with hard-won wisdom and knowledge from survivors, survivor-therapists and therapists. The impact of trauma and how it affects the dynamics of everyday life are clearly and powerfully explained.

The concluding chapter brings together insights, knowledge and expertise in working with survivors, providing clear explanations and guidance for both survivors and therapists to help them navigate the difficult relationship between theoretical knowledge and human understanding of the impact of sexual trauma. The need for a dynamic and genuine alliance between survivor and therapist is clearly explained. The foundations have to be based on mutuality and respect rather than hierarchical and power-based approaches. Therapists are encouraged to bring themselves to the relationship rather than relying only on theoretical therapeutic approaches. Survivors will know when you're being genuine. Also to be mindful of the impact of working with trauma and to integrate self-care into their practice.

There are so many well-made and well-explained learning points, that I wanted to list them all and present them to commissioners, policy makers and funders and say – 'Listen! This is what the problem is, and this is what will help'.

There is much hurt, sadness, betrayal and anger in this book. This isn't a book for the faint-hearted because childhood sexual trauma is at the forefront and centre stage as it needs to be. However, the strength and resilience demonstrated by the survivors and the compassion and care which run like gold thread throughout mean that ultimately, this book is about hope founded on genuine care and respect for survivors.

Fay Maxted OBE
March 2024

Introduction

The nature and legacy of child sexual abuse

Child sexual abuse (CSA) involves forcing or enticing a child or young person to take part in sexual activities, not necessarily involving a high level of violence, whether or not the child is aware of what is happening.

It may involve physical contact, including assault by penetration, or non-penetrative acts such as kissing, rubbing and touching inside or outside clothing. It may also include non-contact activities, such as involving children in looking at, or in the production of, sexual images, watching sexual activities, encouraging children to behave in sexually inappropriate ways or grooming a child in preparation for abuse.

CSA can occur within the family, including extended, blended, foster families or in-laws, and can be perpetrated by male and female adults as well as children, including siblings, step- or half-siblings or cousins. It also occurs outside the family in the larger community, in institutions, children's homes, boarding schools, sports clubs and faith communities, as well as through child sexual exploitation rings and peer-on-peer abuse in gangs. The majority of child sexual abuse is committed by someone known to the child, including peers, neighbours, babysitters, teachers, tutors, sports coaches, priests, ministers or faith leaders (Sanderson, 2013a, 2022).

An under-researched form of CSA is sibling sexual abuse (SSA), which historically has been under-reported. This is in part due to the lack of understanding of what constitutes typical sexual development, and atypical sexual development in which sexual behaviour between siblings is seen as a natural part of sexual experimentation (McCartan, Anning & Qureshi, 2021; Sanderson, 2004, 2022). Many survivors of SSA report that when they have disclosed their abuse to parents or professionals it has been minimized and ascribed to a normal part of sexual development and thus not abusive. There needs to be more research into SSA and CSA committed by children to fully understand the dynamics inherent in this form of abuse and ensure that both the victim and the perpetrator are appropriately supported.

The pervasive nature of CSA is such that it does not just affect the child but has a ripple effect which impacts on families, friends and communities, and which has wider implications for society, the public health service and the criminal justice system. CSA is rarely a one-off event, but more commonly consists of a systematic process which gives rise to a number of dynamics before, during and after the abuse that can add to the impact of the actual abuse.

The process typically starts, before any sexual abuse takes place, through grooming, in which the abuser gains the child's trust by forming a special relationship and makes the child complicit in the abuse in order to reduce the risk of disclosure. During this process, abuse masquerades as love and affection, which distorts the child's reality as it normalizes sexual activity between adults, siblings and children.

A common way to ensnare the child is through play or playing a game that is initially innocuous but evolves over time to become increasingly sexual. As the child engages in the game initially they feel complicit in the game and do not know how to exit from it. If the child resists, the abuser will remind the child that they enjoy playing the game and have not complained before and thus should continue. In addition they emphasize that this is merely a game and that there is nothing wrong with playing games.

The grooming process entices the child into a 'special relationship' with the abuser, while at the same time undermining any attachment to non-abusing parents, caregivers or siblings in the child's life. Making the child feel 'special' is a powerful manipulation, as most children desire to feel 'special' and will enjoy the feeling of 'specialness'. In addition, feeling special can bestow a sense of power and potency on the child, which makes them feel valued. However, this masks the reality of the child's helplessness and powerlessness.

Alongside this, by making the child feel 'special', many abusers actively try to detach the child from their relationship with the non-abusing parent, siblings and other family members. Thus, the abuser inserts doubts into the child's mind about how much they are really loved by the non-abusing parent(s) while simultaneously sowing seeds of doubt in the mind of the non-abusing parent(s) about how much the child can be trusted to be truthful (Sanderson, 2013a, 2015a, 2022).

As a result, both the child and the non-abusing parent(s) are groomed to not trust each other, which reduces the risk of disclosure and the likelihood that the child will be believed. As the bond between the child and the non-abusing parent(s) dissolves, the bond between the child and the abuser is strengthened, making the child more dependent on the abuser in order to avoid them becoming a psychological orphan.

In driving a wedge between the child and their loved ones, the abuser is able to 'divide and rule' and prevent the child from being close to others and disclosing the abuse. In addition, the child's reality is distorted, which prevents them from trusting themselves or the world around them.

In the early stages of the grooming process there is little or no sexual activity as the abuser initially manipulates the child to keep innocent secrets to test the likelihood of disclosure. As the chasm between the child and non-abusing parent(s) widens, and the child becomes more dependent on the abuser, the abuser will begin to initiate sexual contact. This is often so subtle and gradual that the child perceives it as a normal part of a special relationship. As the sexual contact escalates and the child has no other source of secure attachment, they have no choice but to submit.

As the child becomes entrapped, their sense of self and ability to trust and relate to others changes, including how they feel, think and behave. Over time, the child's core identity is changed as they become compliant to please others, or avoid others through withdrawal or hostility, to protect themselves from further abuse (Sanderson, 2013a, 2015a, 2015b, 2022).

As the child withdraws and shuts down, they become more isolated and lose any sense of aliveness. As a result, CSA remains an open wound that can be retriggered throughout their lives, not least whenever they are exposed to CSA-related material, including news coverage and media reporting of CSA.

The abuse of power and distortion of reality can create a trauma bond which binds the abuser and the child together, in which the child loses any sense of self and becomes an extension of the abuser. This is most likely to occur when there is an imbalance of power, when one person has control and authority over another, and when caring and affectionate behaviour alternates with physical, emotional or sexual abuse.

As the core feature of traumatic bonding is that the abuser

is the source of both preserving life and destroying life, the child cannot afford to express rage or anger as this may result in further threat and danger. To manage this, the child has to deny or suppress anger and become compliant and submissive, while directing the anger at themselves or others, such as the non-abusing parent, siblings or other authority figures. The switching between abusive and loving behaviour becomes the 'superglue that bonds' the relationship (Sanderson, 2019).

To manage the contradiction between love and abuse, the child is compelled to seal off any negative beliefs about the abuser and to humanize rather than demonize him or her. In this, the child compartmentalizes the abuse components within the relationship in order to focus on the positive and caring aspects. This necessitates the distortion of reality to override the true nature of the abusive relationship and normalize the abuser's behaviour.

In focusing on the loving aspects of the abuser, the child begins to see the abuser as 'good' and themselves as 'bad'. As the child adapts to the needs of the abuser, they begin to identify with him or her, and start to see the world through the abuser's eyes and adopt his or her beliefs and way of thinking.

In order to protect themselves, the child becomes hypervigilant, living in a persistent state of fear and anxiety. To survive, the child is compelled to 'mind read' the abuser's thoughts, feelings and intentions in order to protect themselves. This means that the child is in a constant state of anticipated threat and hypervigilance. In addition, every time the child has to mind read, they have to come out of their body and inhabit the mind of the abuser, making it harder to feel embodied and hold on to their sense of self.

As the child becomes preoccupied with the needs of the abuser, and significant others, they become increasingly more compliant and acquiescent in order to cater to the abuser's needs and demands, and attempt to gain approval. In order to survive, the child has to surrender their sense of self and adopt the characteristics demanded by the abuser. This leads to developing a 'false' self, in which the child seeks approval through pleasing the abuser by becoming submissive and compliant. This protective survival strategy can derail the development of self and personality, alienate the child from their 'real self' and impair any sense of authenticity or trust in themselves and who they truly are, alongside compromising autonomy and self-agency.

While some abused children do express their anger and hurt through acting out, the majority cannot afford to take that risk for fear of the consequences. The majority need to suppress their anger and rage and thus shut down, becoming hypovigilant or dissociative. Such children are often very pliable and are seen as 'good and well behaved', but the abuse they are experiencing is not recognized.

Over time, the child develops an increasingly higher tolerance for abuse, which can become so entrenched that they are unable to recognize that proximity to the abuser is associated with danger and fear.

These changes in perception are a central feature of many of the distorted core beliefs that survivors of CSA have about themselves and others, and relationships. Ultimately, relationships are no longer places of safety or pleasure but are fraught with terror, anxiety and conflict. This can lead to intense fear of dependency, intimacy and closeness, as well as fear of rejection or abandonment.

To combat these fears, some survivors become compliant and submissive in their relationships while others become aggressive or controlling. Some survivors endeavour to avoid all relationships either by withdrawing from others or exhibiting hostile behaviours that keep others at bay, or they seek refuge in alcohol or drugs as a substitute relationship.

Many of the dynamics seen in traumatic bonding – such as needing to be needed, prioritizing others' feelings over their own, people pleasing and switching between dependency and control – are characteristic of what is commonly referred to as 'co-dependency', but it is important to view such behaviours as survival strategies and a necessary adaptation to CSA.

The legacy of CSA

All too often, a history of CSA underpins a range of issues related to physical and mental health, and is highly correlated with depression, anxiety, post-traumatic stress disorder (PTSD), complex post-traumatic stress disorder (C-PTSD), self-harm, eating disorders, alcohol and drug misuse, and a range of addictions as well as personality disorders (Sanderson, 2013a, 2022). Many survivors are at risk of re-victimization through sexual violence, rape and being enticed into abusive relationships which render them more vulnerable to re-traumatization. The pervasive trauma reactions and emotional dysregulation can lead to anger, lack of control and impulsiveness, and anti-social behaviour. Research indicates that almost 30 per cent of prisoners report experiencing emotional, physical and sexual abuse in childhood (Ministry of Justice, 2012).

The cost of ignoring CSA is high. If survivors are not able to access the treatment they need, they are at risk of becoming heavy service users in different parts of the mental health system, while the underlying trauma is not diagnosed or addressed. It also leads to huge economic and social costs (One in Four, 2019).

Due to the silence, secrecy and shame, the majority of child abuse cases remain hidden and therefore do not enter the criminal justice system. While there is an increase in the reporting of CSA, few offenders are prosecuted and convicted. Around 4 per cent of cases result in someone being charged (Home Office, 2021), and 45 per cent do not progress further due to legal processes.

The narratives in this book are very powerful and at times distressing to read, and yet they all reflect the frightening and confusing experiences of children who have been sexually abused, and how hard it is to break the silence, both as children and later as adults. The stories also attest to their courage and resilience to give voice to and survive the dehumanizing effects of CSA, reconnect to self and others, and make sense of what happened to them.

The purpose of the book

While there is growing awareness and recognition of CSA, it is still extremely hard for survivors to speak out about their experiences. The silence and secrecy inherent in CSA mean that survivors cannot give voice to those experiences. This is compounded by shame and self-blame, which prevents survivors from legitimizing their experience as abusive, or because they were too young, or dissociated, to understand or make sense of what happened to them.

This book provides an opportunity for survivors to describe their personal, unique and direct experiences of CSA. In this, they are acknowledged as experts in their own lives rather than having their experiences constructed or interpreted by researchers or clinicians. These narratives provide unadulterated, first-hand accounts of what happened to them, helping survivors to find their own voice, without professionals trying to direct or reframe how they ought to see themselves, others and the world. In listening to and validating these survivors' accounts, practitioners can have a better understanding of what happened to them, rather than pathologizing them (Johnstone & Boyle, 2018), and can view symptoms as adaptions and accommodations to threat responses and attempts to make sense of these (Boyle & Johnstone, 2020).

Survivors of CSA are not homogenous and vary enormously with regard to their experience of abuse, their age at onset, and its duration, impact, long-term effects and outcome. With that in mind, it is crucial that practitioners can listen and bear witness to each individual experience rather than rely on clinical case studies or theoretical therapeutic formulations.

This acknowledgement of the survivor's experiential expertise is not always reflected in the clinical and research literature. In bearing witness to narratives of lived experiences, clinicians, researchers and service providers are better equipped to make their service delivery more focused, efficient, integrated, culturally appropriate and sustainable. This is vital to ensure that power and control dynamics are not replicated in the therapeutic encounter. The focus must be on equalizing the power dynamics and facilitating empowerment through giving voice. This helps survivors develop confidence and generates feelings of self-worth and a sense of authentic pride in being able to contribute to the healing of others.

Previous reports including accounts from survivors of CSA have shown that, in speaking out, survivors were able to process their experiences more deeply and begin to view themselves in a more empowering and satisfying way. The charity One in Four published *Survivors' Voices: Breaking the silence on living with the impact of child sexual abuse in the family environment*

(2015), which included recommendations for service provision and has been used for training by the NHS as well as in therapeutic training programmes, and *Numbing the Pain: Survivors' voices of childhood sexual abuse and addiction* (2019). The Independent Inquiry into Child Sexual Abuse report *Victim and Survivor Voices from the Truth Project* (2017) and the *Hear Me. Believe Me. Respect Me* survey of adult survivors of child sexual abuse (Smith, Dogaru & Ellis, 2015) also stressed the benefits of allowing survivors to voice their experiences.

Too often survivors are silenced, keeping their secrets because of shame, being unable to speak the unspeakable, fear of being stigmatized or of not being believed or blamed, or fear of perception of others. This book prioritizes their voice and their narrative. While there are many commonalities in these accounts, each experience is unique to each survivor.

In reading the narratives, practitioners will be able to fully hear survivors in their own words, rather than approximations or theory-led case studies. This will enable them to bear witness without pre-judged assumptions and allow them to validate and humanize the survivors' experiences, challenging stereotypes and reducing power imbalances when viewed through the lens of professionals and practitioners. Bearing witness to the unspeakable and actual lived experience is an essential component of healing, as attested to in the words of James Rhodes: 'Being heard, being met with belief, understanding and compassion, feeling safe from judgement, criticism and blame – these things are the absolute key to rebuilding trust and starting the healing process' (2015, p.4).

It is hoped that in bringing greater awareness of the impact of child sexual abuse across the lifespan, it will highlight both the personal as well as the societal consequences. In addition, it is hoped that these narratives will encourage others on their healing journey and inform the wider public of why the impact of CSA in adulthood matters.

How it was done

In early 2019, the author contacted a number of counsellors and therapists specializing in working with survivors of CSA through the charity One in Four to see if any of the survivors they were working with, or had worked with, would be interested in writing about their experiences of CSA. The author also contacted a number of survivors who had contributed to two narrative reports compiled and published by One in Four (2015, 2019), as well as former clients who had previously expressed interest in writing about their experiences. All interested parties were emailed a rationale and outline of the book and offered an opportunity to discuss the project further.

In addition, all the survivors were offered access to support during the writing process, and post writing to manage any triggering and reactivation of trauma. They were also offered a debrief once the writing was complete, although most did not request any further contact. All survivors were given an opportunity to review their narrative prior to final publication. All the survivors were self-selected and as such are not a representative cross-sample of survivors.

The project was interrupted for two years due to Covid-19, which was hard for both the survivors in having the courage to write their accounts and then being unsure when they would be published, and the author in wanting to give a voice to the survivors and having to manage the delay in publication. Throughout, the author's concern was to honour the courage of the survivors in voicing their experiences and that this would be reflected in the publication of the narratives.

The narratives were written by the survivors and practitioners in their own words. In order to retain their authentic voice, the narratives have not been edited except for spelling.

Survivor experts who contributed

Twenty survivors expressed interest and wanted to contribute to the book, although six withdrew as they felt they were not ready to share their story as it was still too raw for them to give voice through a written account that would enter the public domain, despite reassurances that the narratives would be anonymized. It is worth noting that four of the six people who withdrew were survivors of sibling sexual abuse, which supports the evidence that it is often harder to disclose SSA for fear of how that is perceived.

All the survivors who contributed valued the opportunity to give voice to their experiences, although most chose to be anonymous or use a pen name, and were reminded that they could withdraw at any point. All were offered emotional support after writing their narrative. Each narrative details the individual's experience and any views expressed are their own and do not necessarily reflect the views of the author.

Fourteen narratives were chosen, 12 of which were written by survivors (with two of these written from the perspective of survivor practitioners working with survivors of CSA), and two were contributed by practitioners. The majority of survivors were female, with three males, and aged between 30 and 68 years of age. The age of the survivors when the abuse started was from early toddlerhood (*Samia*) through to 16, with one survivor reporting abuse from 11 to 29 years of age (*Maud*).

Most of the survivors were white, including White British and White English, with 14 per cent of the survivors from different ethnic heritages, one South East Asian (*Reena*) and one African Caribbean (*Wallis*). These two both highlighted the need for practitioners to be aware of intersectionality when working with survivors from different cultural and class backgrounds.

Many of the survivors managed to work and have a career, with some survivors going on to train as therapists (*Muriel, Lou, Anthea, Samia, Candice, Reena, Wallis*). It is worth noting that the survivors who contributed to this book are not representative of all survivors, many of whom are unable to work or do not reach their vocational potential due to the long-term effects of CSA.

Who abused them

The abusers included family members such as father (*Muriel, Chris, Samia*), mother (*Maud*), grandfather (*Anthea*) and brother (*Candice*), as well as others outside the family such as a female babysitter (*Samia*), trusted employee of the family (*Alastair*), priests (*Lucy*) and predatory paedophiles (*Matt*). Some experienced multiple abusers (*Muriel, Chris, Lucy, Samia, Matt*). The duration of the abuse varied from brief experiences to 18 years (*Maud*). The CSA rendered a number of the survivors vulnerable to further victimization and sexual violence (*Lou, Samia, Candice*) in adolescence and adulthood.

Disclosure and reporting

A number of survivors attempted to disclose as children but were either not believed or the abuse was minimized, which led to them feeling silenced and being reluctant to disclose later. For some, disclosure and seeking therapy came much

WE ARE STILL HERE

later in life as a result of the re-activation of difficult memories due to media coverage of high-profile CSA cases, in particular Jimmy Savile. A number of survivors did report their abuse to the police (*Lou, Anthea, Chris, Lucy*), sometimes to no avail or more than once, and all felt that this process was protracted.

Experience of therapy

While therapy is an opportunity to give voice, develop a cohesive narrative and construct meaning, many survivors described some negative experiences, especially at the beginning of their journey to healing, in which they were not heard, felt dismissed or were not fully understood (*Anthea, Chris, Samia, Candice*). The most helpful therapies were those that allowed the survivors to give voice to their experiences, where they were heard and believed without judgement or shame (*Muriel, Maud, Matt, Candice*). Some survivors found support, community and a sense of belonging in the 12-Step Programme (*Lou, Matt*), where they felt safe among fellow survivors. (The 12-Step Programme is a recovery programme widely used to help people to overcome substance addictions, behavioural addictions and compulsions, prevent relapse and reclaim a healthy life.)

Definition of CSA

CSA was defined at the start of this introduction to the book. In this context, sexual abuse in the family environment includes being forced or persuaded to take part in sexual activities under the age of 18 by a family member and/or individuals connected to the family, including parents, step-parents, grandparents, primary caregivers, boyfriends or girlfriends of parents, siblings, cousins, uncles, aunts, family friends, babysitters or trusted employees of the family.

Child sexual exploitation (CSE) can be defined as:

> ...a form of child sexual abuse. It occurs where an individual or group takes advantage of an imbalance of power to coerce, manipulate or deceive a child or young person under the age of 18 into sexual activity (a) in exchange for something the victim needs or wants, and/or (b) for the financial advantage or increased status of the perpetrator or facilitator. The victim may have been sexually exploited even if the sexual activity appears consensual. Child sexual exploitation does not always involve physical contact; it can also occur through the use of technology. (Department for Education, 2017)

Structure of the book

While the narratives stand alone, they contain a number of recurring themes which reflect common experiences that survivors have. Chapter 1 consists of the narratives from the survivors and the practitioners. All the narratives were analysed to identify recurring themes across all the survivors with regard to impact. Chapter 2 presents the themes in these narratives and highlights the range of dynamics that practitioners need to be aware of when working with survivors of CSA (Sanderson, 2022). While the narratives highlight the lived experience of survivors of CSA, they also provide insight into what survivors need when they enter therapy, and this is explored in Chapter 3. In addition, insights from other narrative reports are included (Independent Inquiry into Child Sexual Abuse, 2017; One in Four, 2015, 2019; Smith, Dogaru & Ellis, 2015).

Chapter 3 also explores how practitioners can use the Power Threat Meaning Framework, trauma-informed practice and a phased-oriented approach within a relational context to ensure that survivors' needs are met and they can reclaim power and control over their lives.

Use of language

For ease of reading and to avoid the repetition of the gender pronouns he and she, the pronouns they and them are used throughout the book, apart from in the narratives. The terms practitioner, therapist and clinician are used interchangeably to encompass a broad range of professionals working with survivors of CSA.

CHAPTER 1

The Narratives

The survivors: *Muriel, Lou, Anthea, Maud, Chris, Matt,*
                  Lucy, Samia, Candice, Alastair
The practitioners: *Maria, Reena, Jane, Willis*

THE SURVIVORS

Muriel

I was a sexual object in my family. It wasn't spoken about. It certainly wasn't noticed by anyone. I cannot say for sure when it started. I was young. I remember being called a slut by my father as a very young girl. There was just vile bitter judgement in his words. I was the family liar, I was lazy, clumsy and useless. This narrative followed me always. I wonder now if this was to discourage me from disclosing what was happening. I didn't know that the visits to my bed late at night would expand to him sharing me. His brothers and other men would visit the house, or I would be taken and used elsewhere. I can still remember the stench of the box I was kept in sometimes. They would take pictures, polaroids, I would see them on the table, of me and of others. Their thing was pain and humiliation; the more I complained, the more they enjoyed it. There were threats on my life. At night, I would ask God to take me, to remove me from it all. I just wanted to die. I still don't know what my mum thought was happening when I was missing from the house. I don't know why school never questioned my absence. I don't know what the GP was thinking when I was taken for an abortion at about 13 by my dad or why it was okay for my dad to tell the doctor I was a slut. Though the wider abuse lessened as I grew older, my dad made no secret of the fact that he sold my body whenever he needed to, that my only use was as a whore.

I tried to tell my priest around the time of first communion, but instead of helping he refused to allow me to take part in the service I had been preparing for. I was confused and devastated. In the years that followed, I was often physically unwell, having short stays in hospital with bowel problems. I was not able to tell anyone what was happening, but I was able to get respite through illness. I was a teenager with no self-confidence around people. I felt inferior, inadequate, unworthy and spoiled.

I knew I was different by my mid-twenties. I was doing well enough, I had got married, had children, a good career. The abuse did not occupy my thoughts. Marriage had been my escape and the children were everything I wanted them to be. On the surface, it looked fine. There was a pattern of anxiety and depression that badgered me on and off. In my work life I was popular, confident and successful. Outside this, I was depressed, anxious and confused. I was so different in different situations. I had started to notice my memory was faulty though. People around me talked about their schooling with such detail that they knew who they sat next to and the names of teachers, even in primary school. I seemed not to have any of that content. I knew my senior school information was missing as I simply wasn't sent to school much by then, but a lot of other detail of those years seemed sketchy. I didn't understand why I did not know so much of the detail of day-to-day childhood.

I did try to see a therapist at this time, but the session left me feeling a fraud. The therapist told me if I could hold down a job with all that had happened to me there couldn't be much wrong with me, and that their previous client had real problems! As I write this, I can recall their room, the entrance with a steep staircase, but I realize I cannot remember even if they were male or female.

It was only as my daughter moved out of toddlerhood that everything fell apart. It dawned on me that I had married an emotionally unavailable man so had no connection at home to work out what was going on. There had been no intimacy since my daughter arrived. I started to live a compartmentalized and deeply destructive life. In the day, I was an often depressed and anxious mum. I was a successful woman at work, but at night I was making new friends and being someone else altogether! At first this was fun and exciting, but the risks I was taking didn't seem to make much sense. I knew I was attracted to women and not to men, but here I was meeting total strangers, always men, and the worse they treated me the more I went back. I'd hide the bruises and cuts and repeat the whole thing again and again. I started to realize I hated it all, I hated how it made me feel but I didn't seem able to stop. For whole chunks of time, this behaviour took over my life and endangered it.

My depressions grew deeper and lasted longer; for years at a time I kept my night-time life closed down, but every now and then I'd go back to it. I noticed at the same time my daytimes also got out of control. I would leave to go to work in the morning and find myself back home with no idea where I had been all day. There would be messages from work asking where I was, so clearly I had not gone to work. I changed how I worked so that it became easier to cover up these gaps. I have no idea how I made sense of it, but I was expert at covering up. I felt as if I was going mad. Genuinely scared I'd be locked up, I didn't know who to tell. I never let any of the people in parts of my life meet people from other parts, as I knew I was so different in different settings. My work friends would be horrified with who I was at night, and my family would not have recognized how I was with my work friends.

Eventually, I contacted a therapist. I said nothing about what was going on, afraid I'd scare them off. What I wasn't prepared for was the terror that therapy would unlock. My therapist was an analyst and he was mostly silent. I went to therapy to talk, to work it out, and I was mute and so was he! Even now, I don't really know why I kept going back, especially as I got worse, not better. From that first session I was overwhelmed by the sound of a crying baby. As I remained unable to talk, I felt disconnected from my body, and the room I sat in often seemed otherworldly. I felt infectious, as if my story would damage him, and I liked him, so I couldn't get any words out. I think the therapy would have ended as quickly as it started had he not invited me to write to him. I was tainted, damaged, untouchable. His replies were the kindest, most touching things I had ever read. Not only did he believe me but was willing to help.

As therapy progressed, my behaviour and depression became unbearable. I wanted to be dead. The GP referred me to the local mental health team. I was interviewed, and it can only be described as an interview, by an occupational therapist who would not allow me to meet the psychiatrist on duty directly. They were in another room. Each visit ended with me on ever more medication. At one point I was on two

types of anti-depressant, two mood stabilizers and tranquil-
izers. I was no longer living, I floated through life in a haze. I
worry a lot about this period and the effect it must have had
on my children, their mother absent in a drug-induced haze.
Eventually, my GP grew frustrated and I got a referral for a
private psychiatrist who saw me regularly for a while. He
helped me move on to more modern medication, eventually
helping me remove much of what I was taking, and I have
now been medication-free for many years. My diagnosis of
dissociative identity disorder is something I deny as often as
I accept, but my therapist was not fazed by it at all, though
I am sure my refusal to work with it sometimes must have
been irritating. Some sessions were confusing. I would leave
not really remembering what had been said and would need
my therapist to tell me. Dissociating is strange, and knowing
parts of me have had conversations with him is bizarre. I was
lucky that income wise I'd always managed to earn enough to
pay for him, and therapy.

My therapist has been the consistency in my life for more
than a decade, available every week, regardless of my tantrums,
my stuckness, or my confusion. He has let me have extra
sessions when stuff is difficult, and puts up with me ending
sessions early when I throw a strop. He has always behaved as
if he believed me. Even when I could not be sure of the order
of events, he let me try to piece together why I am the way I
am. I am not an easy client. He has consistently let me email
what could not be managed face to face. Since training to be a
therapist myself, I understand that this is extremely unusual,
especially for an analyst!

I started therapy because I wanted to be normal and I knew
I just wasn't the same as everyone else. Getting to normal was
the goal. The noise in my head is hard to explain. There are

voices, separate parts of me that demand their say, but mostly it is noise, background rumblings that get in the way of my thoughts, so it becomes hard to function sometimes. It is similar to having a loud TV on in the background, in another room, distracting and hard to make sense of. The noise is mostly active when I'm stressed. I can lose track mid-sentence of what I am saying. It can be hard to say much at all in group situations in case the noise gets in the way and I appear stupid. One of the hardest things is realizing that getting to 'normal' simply isn't possible. I will always deal with life differently to most people. I still can't sit anywhere where people are behind me; crowded and noisy spaces are not manageable. I still don't sleep through the night and I wonder what the lack of rest is doing to my body. The awkwardness I feel in certain situations will likely be around forever. However, my life is much less compartmentalized. I don't worry about people from different areas of my life meeting. I have connections, friends I love, work I value. I feel cared for, but my core remains lonely and somewhat sad.

In some ways, it is easy to forget about the abuse, that was just stuff that happened and doesn't anymore. It is harder to understand why I was unlovable, what about me is hateful. Why did I get a father who didn't care for me and a mother who to this day feels we have a normal family? I wonder who I would have been had my background been normal, what I might have become, how my relationships would have been. I wonder how my parenting would have been different if I had experienced parents who wanted to meet my needs. My therapist is the closest thing to a caring parent I have ever had and that has to end sometime. The gift he has given me will stay with me always though. I trust more people, I enjoy most days, I have interests and a home. It is likely that without therapy I would be dead, and my children would be deeply hurt.

Lou

It was both breathtaking and bewildering to realize at 50 that my childhood sexual abuse required a lot more metabolizing and dissolving within my system than I ever had believed previously.

For more than two decades, from my thirties to my fifties, I'd been under the impression that I'd done all the work necessary on my early trauma. In fact, I'd spent all of my initial training in the personal development field in neuro linguistic programming (NLP) and hypnotherapy, doing processing work on my CSA, or so I thought. I then went on to train as a psychotherapist, doing even more personal attachment and trauma work in overcoming my history, with both talk therapy and other forms of holistic body work.

I always knew the CSA was there, sat underneath my other presentations of addiction, my eating disorder, even the psychosis I went through in my mid-twenties. The trauma seeped through everything, tainting and fuelling the self-loathing that comes alongside any kind of abuse. I mean, why treat yourself well when there's a part of you that feels damaged, disgusting, dirty, wrong? The addiction, the food, the other self-destructive strategies work well to keep the traumatized part in its place, repressed, hidden, at bay and way out of consciousness, for a while at least. Running around in a busy world being semi-conscious, constantly on sugar, alcohol and keeping the adrenalin flowing worked for a while! But not for long.

However, moving into my thirties it wasn't as if I was averse to doing the trauma work. Finally, I stopped running, became a therapist and trained primarily in addiction. It was later that I realized most addictions are absolutely rooted in trauma, so I began to diversify and look far more into that. The interesting point to make is that I actually took many of my clients through the journey of overcoming their childhood sexual abuse; these were mainly the clients who turned up at my door. Often, I was taking them to the police station to report the abuse, to help them walk towards their fears in order to help them begin to get their voices back.

But I was unware of my own inner landscape. I never thought it was me who needed to do that trip to the police station. After all, in my mind, I'd done the work, hadn't I? My CSA was not holding me back I didn't think, and besides, I always said to myself, my abuse wasn't really that bad. I mean, compared to some of my clients it was barely anything, for goodness sake.

I was four, maybe five, when my abuse happened. It was a female for a start, so for years I joked about it when I told people and laughingly said, 'Well, at least it didn't put me off men!' But at 53, I've still not had any long-term relationships of significance, even after all the years of therapy. So whether abuse is from a male or a female, it still has an effect on your sexuality and ability to be intimate for sure. I also used to say to myself, well, my abuse didn't go on for ages, I don't even know how many times it happened – but time length doesn't matter, abuse is abuse. The other way I would minimize it was by saying that at least she wasn't a member of my family, so I always discounted it next to other people's abuse by their uncles, fathers, mothers. My abuser was just a young caretaker; she was a late teenager and probably didn't even know what she was doing. But then I got raped in my teenage years too, and I also made light of the rape. I think there was a pattern occurring of not really making it into much so I didn't have to deal with it. I told myself that the rape didn't really count either, because I was drugged and given Rohypnol. So, for years I made out that my conscious mind didn't remember it so the event didn't really lodge in my system. How wrong was I? Of course, my unconscious mind had totally remembered it. In group therapy, at the well-known rehabilitation centre I worked at three decades later, I remember vividly when a client sat next to me in group and shared for the first time a remarkably similar story. I have never known a bodily experience like it. Nor have I been through one since. I had a massive trauma reaction, went into meltdown and had to leave the group so I could allow myself to sob, shake and shiver back in the staff room – trauma activation at its most severe.

But back to what I was saying at the beginning about how CSA and sexual trauma takes more work than a few NLP sessions or a while of talk therapy because it lives in the body and takes time to get to and fully release ourselves from.

I say that because even after all the work I'd done on myself, in my fifties, I had a bit of an awakening. My wake-up call was ovarian cancer. I went into hospital immediately and had a full hysterectomy and afterwards decided to do some personal journeying yet again, alongside some holistic treatments. I decided to go on a deep dive retreat with a lady who had healed her own stomach cancer. It was a little like inner journalling, an exploration of travelling down through the outer layers into the body and finding one's core self, deep within. And during that guided process, an old memory emerged. It was the memory of the young caretaker. I was gobsmacked, I thought I'd done all the processing I'd needed too, but finally, I also realized that the emotional component to it, and the sadness and loss, hadn't completely gone.

What followed was a further trauma healing EMDR (eye movement desensitization and reprocessing) journey, and part of the journey was also me finally reporting it to the police. I reported not only the childhood sexual abuse but the teenage rape as well. I needed to deal with three different police forces, which was slightly disconcerting, but the main one I dealt with on the childhood stuff was absolutely brilliant. What I couldn't quite comprehend was the sheer amount of emotional energy yet to be released. When I spoke to the police and did my video interview, it astounded me how much I actually sobbed, knowing that I had done so much work on myself previously. In fact, over the decades, I'd engaged in so many forms of therapy, healing and trauma work and yet here I was still unable to get my breath. It gave me even more compassion for the survivors I treat and work with in coming forwards and reporting their own abuse.

I felt there was something extremely powerful for me about being able to speak to a hierarchical figure, such as a police person, and have them fully believe me. I don't think it helped my journey at all hearing from a close member of my family, while I was in EMDR therapy, who said to me, 'Why on earth are you doing that? If it (the abuse) had bothered you that much, you would have told somebody about it at the time!' Isn't it amazing that some people can't see how a child of that age is totally unable to speak out or find their voice? It is so sad that sometimes family members, like previously when the abuse was occurring, can't be available emotionally. It's their own guilt I guess. It also helps to explain that with no one available emotionally, no wonder we hide it and hold it all in.

Now, I don't want you to go away thinking if you don't share or do work on your trauma story, you'll end up getting cancer! That's not what I mean. The cancer was a pointer for me to go back into the body and look again, and go deeper this time. To release the last remnants of shame and get back my voice, which I'd never had in my four decades on the planet. It was also about having a DNA chain within my family on my mum's side, where sadly all the female side succumb to cancer, so it's not all trauma-led. But that helped me look again within myself for sure.

And I'm glad it did because since doing the final therapeutic process and EMDR and the reporting of it, I'm now finally able to fully speak about my rape and my CSA and share my truth. I'm even able to stand on stage in front of many other people and tell the story, without any concern or undue worry about how others may see me or judge me, just a message to say to them, go towards your own stuff! Because it doesn't sadly just magically go away.

I love the fact that I can finally get fully involved in helping others who have experienced similar sexual trauma. I can say to them, it doesn't matter when or how you do the work, just follow the pointers and go towards what draws you. For me, now, I'm a great believer in EMDR of course. But there are other methods and modalities that have a lot of value in them too. And again, one of the main differences, for me, is in the relationship with the therapist or the person helping you. I did see somebody briefly for EMDR who unfortunately not only seemed to suffer with narcolepsy and kept nodding off in our sessions, she also frequently forgot the name of the young caretaker, the abuser – a serious mistake to make with a survivor.

Whatever modality of healing or person or people we choose to be on our recovery journeys, what we really, really need is above all to feel fully heard, totally listened to, absolutely acknowledged and vehemently validated. Because that doesn't happen when we are young and going through it and we need it now, whether it's 20, 30 or 40 years later.

I hope my story has been helpful and I'm sending you much

courage and faith on your healing journey too. We do get 'there' wherever 'there' is in the end!

Anthea

The sexual abuse began in the 1970s. I was approximately seven years old and the perpetrator was my so-called maternal grandfather, who continued abusing me periodically for four to five years.

There is no word to aptly describe the fear I experienced in those traumatic years whenever we had to dutifully visit or endure visits from our grandparents, especially when being 'babysat'.

During that time, I remember my childlike inner dialogue, 'Am I safe or will he try to touch me today? How can I avoid him without upsetting him?'

Or I would be in complete denial and pretend he was a loving, doting granddad, go to him for cuddles or go on the camping and fishing trips, only for my innocent, childlike hopes to be shattered.

One day, while on one of our dutiful visits, I was sat on his knee in our grandparents' front room. He attempted in a room full of various family members to abuse me again. Somehow I mustered enough strength to utter a pleading whisper, 'Grandaaaad'. His response was to tell me to shush.

After that day, he never tried to abuse me again.

When sharing my story, I never refer to him as Grandfather; he does not deserve that title.

Aged 15, I disclosed the abuse to my parents, and although they believed me, what followed next may be hard for some to read but heartbreakingly common for many survivors, and especially true of the 1980s.

As with many victims I was silenced, a powerless child who had no choice but to continue with the obligatory visits until many years later when in my early thirties I made an informed decision, with the support of my therapist and husband, to cut him from my life.

To no longer be manipulated by the man who had abused me was my first real taste of freedom.

This was one of the first empowering experiences I had, to sever those heavy chains that had kept me linked to him and under his control, but a lot was to happen before that day came.

Although the sexual abuse ended before I hit my teens, the abuse didn't stop there. I, as well as my parents, were bullied and manipulated by him and his family into silence; we were to forgive, forget and carry on with life as 'normal'. After all, that's what you're supposed to do, isn't it?

Before we erased him from our family videos and photo albums, onlookers would never guess what was going on behind closed doors. All very neatly swept under that mat! I felt like the mat – I, the child, was the one hiding it all and being trampled on.

I was often asked by his family members, 'Why didn't you stop him? Why didn't you say no? Why didn't you tell somebody? Why did you have to say anything at all?' Manipulative questions a child is unable to answer. Never was he asked, why did you abuse Anthea? So it never occurred to me to ask why he had hurt me.

Instead, I asked myself the same questions the adults had been asking me. The self-blame and shame began.

With crocodile tears, he had manipulated my parents into believing that he was the innocent one, with the following lies,

'I didn't do it on purpose, it must have happened when we were playing. Perhaps I touched her there by accident when I tickled her.' My mum was desperate to believe this and maintain a relationship with her father, as she was a 'Daddy's girl', he often told her, and Mum didn't want to lose that crown.

So I had no choice but to continue seeing him, and what followed was an endless nightmare full of triggers: a song, the decorations on his wall, his hands, certain smells, topics of specific conversations and places. The fear and trauma felt endless.

My dad promptly put an end to his eldest daughter being left alone with his monster father-in-law; he was to never have the opportunity to sexually abuse me again. It didn't occur to my poor parents and no one advised them that the best thing for their daughter would be for her to never have to see him again.

It was then suggested by our church leader that I could regularly visit an older female member of the church I was attending at the time of my disclosure. I had already formed an attachment with her and, though I was grateful for her gentle listening ear, how could she be expected to support a young teen who was living in a confusing, tormented world full of trauma, depression, shame, flashbacks and dissociation? We were both out of our depth but muddled our way through those chats, with her having no clue how to tackle the mess that was sat opposite her in floods of tears. She tried to help the only way she knew how and that was to pray, but prayer is by no means an instant wave of a non-existent magic wand to heal psychological trauma.

There was little validation and no professional support provided for me at the time of the disclosure and this continued to be the case until I had my breakdown aged 30.

There was a devastating lack of awareness of the impacts of childhood sexual abuse in society and in those around me. It was inevitable that at some point in the future I would no longer be able to maintain the façade of having a perfect life.

Close friends knew I was a victim of sexual abuse; however, this was not a term I really heard at the time; more often than not it would be 'he touched you inappropriately'.

A question I was often asked was: 'How have you survived? How are you still here?'

In my mid twenties, I confided in a friend, trying to articulate how I was feeling, having no comprehension of the impacts of abuse. I shared with her I felt sad, tearful, lost, lonely and depressed but confused as to why. My friend's automatic response was to say, 'But you have it all, a wonderful husband, two lovely children, a supportive family, a home, job, car and nice holidays.' I didn't take offence, as she was trying to remind me of how blessed I was, and to onlookers I could see how it would appear ever so rosy on the surface. Though I knew this not to be her intent, the conversation ended with me feeling hopeless and ungrateful. 'I am a complete failure, I "should" be happy, shouldn't I?'

But I continued to keep busy with creating the 'perfect life'. My coping mechanism was to dissociate, and bury and hide the pain. I was working hard to create something in my life I didn't believe I was worth. I was wearing a mask and believing my own lies that everything was fine, and hoping that I was successfully hiding my feelings of inadequacy and worthlessness to the world around me.

For years after the abuse I muddled through life as best as I could until I was 30. Throughout the 80s and 90s it didn't occur to anyone, myself included, that I was such a troubled soul. All the signs of being a victim of sexual abuse were there but I internalized my 'failings' and put them down to it being my fault, that I was just odd and not 'normal'.

My abuser's behaviour had taught me that I had no purpose other than to be used, that my life held no value and my voice was of no consequence. 'If my granddad can do "that" to me, I must be worthless.' This defined my future and self-perception; he was holding up a mirror and all I could see was a little girl who was dirty and bad. She had grown into an adult body but was still bad, gagged and of no significance. It was a dark world but it was my dark world, I had learnt to live in it, it was familiar and felt strangely safe.

I was unaware that this denial would take me to a day when I would attempt to end my familiar, 'safe' world.

Years of imploding, living in silent torment, had finally taken its toll and I tried to end all the mental torture by jumping out of my parents-in-law's bedroom window. My husband, children and I had temporarily moved in with them as I could no longer cope with running the home and raising my family. I was swiftly admitted to a secure mental health unit.

What then followed was four years of intermittent admissions to the mental health ward, and other suicide attempts. I received the controversial electroconvulsive therapy (ECT); the doctors had tried other interventions but I was considered too at risk because of the suicide attempts. I received ECT, occupational therapy, cognitive behavioural therapy and eventually psychodynamic therapy in the years that followed.

I began to slowly put the dots together and make sense of what, up to that point, had defined me.

I had made some changes with the support of the professionals but it was just the beginning of the road of self-discovery, healing and hope.

In 2011, I embarked on a course to train as a qualified therapeutic counsellor, and part of the course required us to self-examine and evidence in our journals our self-awareness learning.

When I take a look through the four years' worth of thick folders, I observe a youngish woman who was still in a lot of pain, despite overcoming a debilitating breakdown, but there are pages upon pages of lightbulb moments and revelations of why I am who I am. I also gained an understanding of my learnt behaviours and where they had come from. I wrote them down, shared my learning with my husband and peers, then set myself goals to change them, determined to no longer be the victim. It was at college I discovered Carl Jung and his quote 'I am not what has happened to me, I am who I choose to become'.

I was erasing those negative automatic thoughts one by one.

'I am ugly' changed to 'I am beautiful'.

'No one loves me' changed to 'I am loved and lovable' and so on.

I had post-it notes hidden round my home, and some not so hidden, so I could be reminded every day that I get to choose how I see myself. I no longer have to see myself through the eyes of the abuser.

He had blinded me. I could not see my potential, but removing his eyes and his voice removed the darkness and shed light on the real me.

No longer would I minimalize what had happened to me; instead, with hard work, I formed healthy boundaries and built a firm foundation for a new life where I no longer had to live in his dark shadows. There truly is light at the end of that tunnel.

Around the time of my training, I reported him to the police, resulting in his name being on the Sex Offenders Register for two years.

When that was all over, he still continued to spill his lies, so I decided to make one last trip to his home, after which there would be no more obligatory, disempowering visits. I stood in his front room for the last time, tall and empowered, and my husband, sister and dad stood quietly beside me and listened on with pride as they witnessed their loved one put an end to his abuse.

The adrenaline kicked in and after years of imploding I was finally exploding, all in his direction and rightly so. At last I was angry. I didn't shout, kick and scream but remained calm, and this enabled me to say all that I had intended.

From that day until he deceased, we never heard from him again.

Maud

From an early age, I was always looking for something – I didn't know what it was but it was something. I always felt lost and alone, even within my family and friends, at school and at parties. Although I had a brother and two sisters, I never felt connected to them. I was always the 'and' – brother one, sister one, sister two and me. Even though I was the third child I felt I was the 'and'; wherever I went, I was found tagging along at the back.

It wasn't until recently, at the ripe old age of 64, that I realized what it was I was searching for and how this has been offered to me through the years by my therapist. I didn't realize that what she offered me was the part that my mother couldn't, or wouldn't, give to me – she listened. All my life, I blamed myself for not being heard or understood, feeling that there was something wrong in my communication and that my mother was trying hard to understand but I was preventing her from hearing me.

What was confusing was that she seemed to be available to my siblings, especially my younger sister. She was more than able to listen and respond to her and be available whenever she was needed. My mother made sure that my younger sister's needs were met at all times even if it meant ignoring my or my other siblings' needs. Even as I write this, I am consumed with guilt and fear of my mother's reaction to these words despite the fact that she has been dead for 30 years. If she were able to read this, she would be furious and blame me for being selfish and spoilt.

This was the pattern of my life until I was a teenager, when I was sent to a psychiatrist to find out what was wrong with me. I had missed out on most of my school years and was absent for huge chunks of time. Finally, the truant officer came calling and my mother blamed me for not going to school. As a result, I had to go to court, was put on probation, allocated a social worker and sent to a psychiatrist. Despite all these professionals being involved no one was able to work out why I was absent from school.

No one asked me and I could not tell them. I was silenced by my mother and terrified to tell the truth – that my mother was sexually abusing me. Each morning before school she would call me to come to her bed on the pretence of wanting to be comforted. Her insistent pleading and calling for me meant I had no choice but to comply by going to her. The psychiatrist sensed that there was something unhealthy in my relationship with my mother but I couldn't tell him that as my mother said I would be seen as crazy and sent to an institution. So I lied and defended her to protect her, as the only time I felt any closeness to her was when she was sexually intimate with me.

I was not able to tell anyone, and the abuse continued until I was in my late twenties.

So although I gained some closeness to my mother, it was at a huge cost. I can now see how this has affected me in terms of not gaining an education, never being able to have a relationship, or children, or family, and being absolutely terrified of people. I am even scared of my therapist, despite the fact that she is the one and only person I truly trust and can be honest with. All my life I have been too scared to live and feel sad that I can't have relationships with others, including my siblings. Because of the lack of trust in professionals and the number of counsellors who tried to help but couldn't listen and didn't understand, I started to self-harm and play Russian roulette with my life – mixing alcohol with medication, stepping in front of traffic, not wanting to be here but being too scared to take my own life.

My first psychiatrist sensed there was something wrong but did not take action. I would have stopped him as I feared the consequences of the abuse coming out and being punished by my mother. I couldn't afford to upset my mother so I had to put him off the scent by telling him how wonderful my mother was. In writing this, I can't help wondering what would have happened if I had been able to open up to one of the many professionals who saw me – would they have been able to stop the abuse, would I have been safe, or would my mother's prediction have come true and I would have ended up in a psychiatric institution? I wonder, would I have married, would I have had children?... As it is, I have never been able to form a relationship with anyone. If I had been able to trust and found the right person, would I have been able to live more?

All I can say is that when I found the right therapist who gave me time and patience and allowed me to push boundaries without judgement and kept me safe, I slowly began to trust for the first time ever. Despite pushing boundaries endlessly and sometimes cruelly, my therapist remained constant and consistent. At times, I despised her for this and became furious with her for not showing me the door, rejecting me or giving up on me. At times, it felt it would have been easier had she done so as that would be proof that my mother was right, that I was the crazy one who was unlovable and did not deserve to be cared for. I still occasionally struggle to understand how my therapist can listen to me and be there for me when the one person who should have been able to do that didn't.

All I ever wanted to do was to live and trust my mother and she abused that. She also prevented me from having a relationship with my father, which is something I didn't realize until after she died. Through therapy, I realized that by having to keep this secret and to lie stopped me from being close to my father and my siblings for fear that the secret would come out. What has struck me writing this is that through the sexual abuse I was prevented from receiving care and affection from my family, which has left me with a huge sense of emptiness and aloneness all my life that I have never been able to fill, despite the alcohol and medication. Now finally, in my mid-sixties, I am in a better place, and although the emptiness and loneliness are still there they are not as big and I am more able to accept myself and have started to actually like myself at times. I now realize that it is the shame of the abuse and what my mother did that has crippled me, not because I am flawed or defective. I am finally beginning to make some sense of a world that has always been confusing, where I have known and not known that there is something wrong.

It has taken me a long time to get here and to realize that my whole life was lived in a fog of dissociation in which I was constantly confused and uncertain. Finally, the fog is lifting and I have days of clarity and waking up and thinking I am glad to be here and I appreciate being alive. I have stopped continually searching for the lost part as I have finally found what I have been looking for all my life – my voice. After all these years of keeping silent, pushing people away and hiding my shame, I have finally found my voice and have been heard. Not every day is great and there are pockets and moments of difficulty, but overall I am glad to be here.

I believe that the unstinting support from my therapist in wanting to hear my voice and now me writing this is a testament to finding my voice, which is allowing me to be human and listened to. I have finally found my voice and want to sing each day.

Chris

The impact of being a victim and survivor of all forms of abuse still lives on within me and has shaped me to be the person I am. To this day, I am still on a journey of recovery and growth.

I am one of six siblings. I grew up in three domestic violent households and we all suffered mental, emotional, physical abuse and neglect. Some of us suffered sexual abuse within and external to the family. There is generational abuse on both my mum and dad's side of the family.

Between 1970 and 1977 I lived with my biological mum and dad (Mum left due to domestic violence and Dad having affairs). I personally cannot remember much of the first seven years of my life other than being introverted and being a good little girl. If I was good, my parents wouldn't fight, would they?

Between 1977 and 1981 I lived with my dad and step-mum (Dad went to prison for paedophilia and my step-mum starved and abused us). My dad had an affair with this woman while being with my mum. He later married her. She had seven daughters. My dad was convicted of sexual abuse of some of her girls. When he went to prison, my step-mum's abuse of us escalated. My mum lost touch with us when we moved to Wales and lived in a tent, but when we came back to England, my mum instigated access and custody proceedings. The battles between the adults, using us children as the pawns, were truly painful and made us grow up very quickly.

Between 1981 and 1986 I lived with my mum and step-dad (my step-dad was an alcoholic). When we went back to live with Mum we thought all our abuse was over. Unfortunately, she had married another abusive person who was also an alcoholic. We lived on a council estate and we were on benefits – he would demand money from Mum to fuel his drinking at the expense of us. My mum was completely under his control and so were we. We all left home just before our 16th birthdays; the police could not take us back home as they had previously when we had run away.

Even in death, my step-dad controlled the situation. I missed my mum dying by an hour because he would not tell me which hospital she was in. My sister and I could not go to her funeral because of the ongoing police case.

Over the last four decades we have reported the abuse we have suffered to our schools, the social services and to the police but each time we were either not believed or the appropriate action was not taken. In 2016, we went to the police again and even now – at the time of writing – our family case is still proceeding through the Criminal Justice System.

The impact on me (and my siblings) has been far reaching.

I spent the first 15 years of my life enduring chronic abuse and neglect. I spent the next 15 years trying to make myself a 'somebody'. I had been told all my life that I was a 'nobody'. I wasn't happy with this label and I thought I could change it. I hid my true identity from everyone I met as an adult; I didn't trust people. Would they judge and hurt me too? To them, I was happy, smiley, kept my head down and got on with my job. If I kept silent about my past, if I kept it a secret, all would be okay! Wouldn't it?

I did this for 15 years and was successful at it. If someone asked me a question about my past life I would evade answering it.

At the age of 28, the cracks started to show. I had my son, and this was the first time that my past had truly caught up with me. My brain couldn't reconcile the love I felt for my child and the child abuse I had suffered at the hands of my parents and step-parents.

I was cleaning my son's genitals one day when I had an overwhelming feeling that I might be abusing him – his nappy was a real messy one and I had spent a lot of time cleaning him. I went to my doctor and asked, 'Am I an abuser?' My GP asked me about my past and I told him the bare minimum and he said, no, it was absolutely normal thinking for what I had been through, and he recommended some counselling for me. Hearing him say those words to me was a huge relief.

For the next 18 months, I felt my mental health sliding. (I didn't know this at the time.) I just knew I wasn't coping very well... I was trying to juggle a full-time job as the financial controller of a medium-sized company, my toddler and my past life.

I was becoming more and more overwhelmed and feelings of anger, sadness, anxiety, depression and bereavement were showing up in my life.

My mum had left the family home when I was seven and I was left to be the mini-mum to my siblings.

From the age of 15 to 30, my siblings came to me with all their problems and I had to try and deal with the impact of the child abuse we had suffered. Again, I didn't know what I was doing at the time; we all just tried to get on with life the best way we knew how.

At the age of 30, I was in the office working on an Excel spreadsheet when the numbers starting jumping out at me. I ran into the main office saying the numbers were attacking me. At this time in my life I was being bullied at work, I had an excessive workload, was working very long hours and suffering from immense guilt about my child being in full-time nursery. After my 'breakdown' at work I was sent home and was referred to counselling again. I asked my doctor not to put anything on my records pertaining to mental health issues because it would affect my chances of promotion. We put my current conditions down to work stress.

My GP referred me to the counselling service but there was a long waiting list and I needed immediate help. The occupational health advisor was able to get my company to pay for private therapy sessions for me. I had six sessions. Each session was the same – I drove there, I sat in a chair, the counsellor said nothing, I cried my eyes out. Nothing was said about the child abuse I had suffered or the current situation I found myself in. I was not asked any questions and I didn't offer any information. This was probably the first time I had cried like this and now I can see it was a huge release for me. All that stored-up chronic stress from anger, sadness and loss.

All I knew at the time was that my self-esteem was at rock bottom. I couldn't shake off how I was feeling.

I eventually got a job working at a psychiatric hospital as

their finance manager. I soon realized that the patients in the hospital were worse off than me; I was coping quite well and had been through worse than some of the inpatients. Throughout my life, I had turned to fitness to manage my anger and to make me feel better. I saw there was a need for the inpatients to do fitness to lift their mood and to give them energy. I qualified as a fitness instructor after having my second child and introduced a fitness service into the hospital. I was at the hospital for 11 years and loved what I did.

However, all this time I felt as if I had been hiding my true self from the world. I had lost my identity. All my life I had been ashamed of who I was, where I came from. Running away from this, hiding from this, keeping up appearances was exhausting.

- I had to be the best accountant (it took me eight years to qualify because studying was difficult).
- I had to be the best mother (my son being in full-time nursery made me feel I was failing as a mother).
- I had to have a clean house all the time (this was impossible with a child but I tried my hardest).
- I had to be there for everyone else (it made me ill).
- I had to keep a smile on my face (everything would be okay).

I had an overwhelming desire to share my experiences with others, to break the silence, to share what my siblings and I had been through and to give other victims and survivors hope that there is life after abuse.

So in 2012, I wrote a book about my life. Each of my siblings wrote a chapter too.

So far, I have talked about the impact on my mental health but not my physical health and my relationships.

As a child, I felt terror, especially when the shouting started, or when my step-dad would come home from the pub on a Sunday drunk and turn the food table upside down while the football was playing in the background. To this day, I have issues about sitting at a dinner table on a Sunday and football.

I felt the shame of having a paedophile as a dad, especially when a child called it out in the playground – I didn't know what a paedophile was but it made me feel different and dirty.

I felt the guilt of not being able to save my siblings and my mum from being beaten and abused. On many occasions, I felt the anger rising up in me but had to suppress it because the adults had all the power and the control. I learnt that if I voiced my opinion or showed a flicker of expression on my face, I would be beaten. I have actually lost control of my anger twice in my life and I didn't like it. It scared me into getting help.

It's only now, after many years of trauma counselling, that I have acknowledged that I was let down by many people and I have allowed myself to understand that my anger is justified. Over the years I managed to channel my anger into keeping my family together and change things for me, them and other survivors.

During my teenage years, I used to run long distances and undertake fitness sessions to help me manage my anger. The music and the fitness used to make me feel good and calmer. When I had overwhelming stress, I used to purge and make myself sick. It was almost as if I was cleansing myself from the inside out. I tried to be perfect to have a sense of control. In my school work, if I made a mistake I would rip the page up and re-write it, many times. I also kept my home environment immaculate. I didn't really socialize and if I had someone around to the house for a cuppa I couldn't wait for them to go, wash their cup up and restore my house again. This calmed me down.

When I had my breakdown in my thirties, my periods stopped for a while because of chronic stress. I had secondary fertility issues because of this.

In my forties, I had four hip operations including two hip replacements from osteoarthritis. I believe that this was down to the chronic stress and poor nutrition as a child and my lifestyle as an adolescent and adult. I have had two anal surgeries due to the chronic stress and constipation I suffered from experiencing domestic violence as a child and teenager, and the child abuse I endured.

Smears are hard for me to undertake – at my last smear this year I had to ask for someone to hold my hand and soothe me so I wouldn't become triggered while the procedure was carried out by the nurse. Throughout the smear, I cried silent tears. At the age of nine I had an internal examination at the police station – even though I told them the man hadn't touched me there they wanted to double check. They hurt me physically and this has triggered me all my life.

Throughout my lifetime, I have endured cold sores, which always manifest in times of stress and now I have to take tablets to manage the outbreaks. I have suffered from hyperarousal and hypervigilance. When I hear children crying or angry voices I have to investigate and on many occasions I have stepped in, sometimes at a huge cost to me. I am very aware of my surroundings, I pick up on everything subconsciously and it's exhausting. I have suffered from flashbacks and nightmares, especially during the criminal justice process over the last four years. I used to be told off at school for not concentrating and I now know I was dissociating; I was more worried where my next meal was coming from than what I was being taught. Even now as I an adult when I become highly stressed I cannot take things on board, I do not retain information and it can make studying extremely hard, but not impossible!

As a family we have been devastated – Mother's day, Father's day, birthdays, Christmases are often difficult. As siblings, we have come together as adults and our case is currently being investigated 30 years after it happened. This again will be traumatizing and there is no specialist support readily available – we have to pay for our therapy.

As a result of decades of chronic stress on my body, every time I have been in for surgery I become traumatized and highly stressed, making recovery hard. Once the anaesthetist pulled my gown down quickly without telling me what was happening to put on the electrodes, and I became triggered and burst into tears and then I had to explain to a complete stranger what was happening. There are many more examples I can share but I do not have the word count here to do so. I have found that most health professionals do *not* understand the impact of child sexual abuse on victims and survivors and in my opinion they all need trauma training.

Matt
A Journey of Healing, Copyright Matt Carey Books, www.mattcareybooks.com

It took me many years to openly admit that I am a survivor of child sexual abuse. Like almost all survivors, I was too ashamed, scared, traumatized to tell anyone what had happened – not my parents, friends or family.

When I was eight years old, I was targeted by a group of predatory paedophiles who subjected me to 18 months of horrific sexual abuse in the public toilets of local parks and on the seafront of my hometown.

Based on the number of locations I can now remember, 13 all told that I can recall, and the fact that there were always at least two but usually three men involved each time, I was probably sexually abused, molested or raped at least 30 times.

The men worked in rotation; while one would abuse me, another would either hold me or stand close by, and a third was a look out, in case we were disturbed – which happened a few times. They made me feel that I was entirely responsible for what happened. They behaved as if they were entitled to do what they were doing; it was their right and they convinced me that it was ALL my fault.

The menace, the unrelenting pressure, the fear and shame I felt, the threats to my life…were far worse than the actual physical sexual abuse that took place. I couldn't see any way out, I felt completely trapped and so I shut down – mentally, emotionally – and just went along with it. As a means of survival, I submitted to and normalized the abuse.

This behaviour was the source of my deepest shame throughout much of my adult life, and one which during my teenage years and in my early twenties, I would taunt myself with verbally, and physically by punching myself in the face whenever the PTSD was triggered.

As soon as the abuse had finished, I buried the horrific memories so deep inside me I could barely remember anything that had happened – until, aged 12, I reached puberty, which triggered off relentless and savage memory flashbacks to the abuse. There was suddenly a deep, visceral feeling of horror inside that was overwhelming. I felt dirty, ashamed and disgusted with myself but I didn't have enough visual memory to understand exactly why.

On the surface, at the beginning, I projected to the world that everything was fine; I could flick a switch in my mind and 'act' so that no one knew what was really going on. But I was scared of being attacked and of being humiliated; I became very anxious, depressed and often paranoid about other people's intentions.

To put it simply, the abuse psychologically and emotionally crippled me for many years – I avoided all physical, emotional and sexual intimacy for most of my adult life, such was the long-term, ongoing trauma of the abuse.

I started drinking regularly in my mid-teens, and while I hated the taste, the effect throughout my body was sensational. I cannot understate how amazing alcohol was for me when it worked – it felt like a chemical reaction surging through me, and I felt ALIVE in a way that I never had before.

But these feelings of euphoria didn't last and soon getting to oblivion was the only way to drown the horrific feelings and savage, obsessive thoughts of self-hatred. At my worst, I drank Old Spice Aftershave and would punch myself in the face as I screamed obscenities at myself in front of the mirror. I wanted to see myself hurting, such was my shame and self-hatred.

I hit rock bottom aged 20 years and in March 1993 I went to my first Alcoholics Anonymous (AA) meeting. Thanks to AA, I haven't had an alcoholic drink since. This was the crucial turning point in my life, although I didn't know it at the time. In AA, I greatly benefitted from the experience, strength and hope of those who had walked the path before me – alcoholics who had stopped drinking and had successfully embraced a sober, productive life.

Crucially, a number of these inspirational members, I soon learned, were also survivors of sexual abuse.

With their gentle guidance and encouragement, I was soon attending daily AA meetings and twice weekly trauma therapy sessions with an amazing life teacher. He was a remarkable man, a semi-retired clinical psychologist with a passion for holistic therapy. He was also a deeply spiritual man, and over time, as I very tentatively learned to trust him, I found him to be truly inspirational.

He was the first professional I spoke to about the abuse, but the trauma therapy did not start straight away. He began by teaching me simple concentration techniques to help me to deal with the regular panic attacks, the disassociation and the horrific flashbacks to the abuse that were triggered by the PTSD.

He helped me to understand what the hell was going on when I was triggered – I learned what my triggers were, and what it meant to go into shock when I had been triggered; I started to recognize the fight or flight syndrome. As horrifying as these experiences were, they helped me to develop a cognitive understanding of what was happening in my mind and to my body when I was triggered.

After a while, the trauma therapy started, and I told him in as much detail as I could then remember about what had happened to me. The sessions were overwhelming and exhausting, but a vitally important beginning to my journey of healing. They helped create a firm foundation to my recovery, but they were only a beginning, nonetheless.

Beyond these traditional therapy sessions, he also taught me how to communicate again through role playing and drama; he encouraged me to meditate; he inspired me to connect with nature as a way to come out of my crazy head and a mind that was often savage with PTSD flashbacks – and he impressed on me the importance of developing a sense of worth, of getting involved with the community, of feeling useful.

During the next few years this structured approach to my recovery – the balance between daily AA meetings, regular contact with fellow survivors of abuse who were further along the healing journey than I was, and weekly trauma therapy sessions – was absolutely vital to my overall healing. However, I have needed intensive trauma therapy a number of times since – in my late twenties, mid-thirties and early forties – when the PTSD has been especially traumatic.

My mid-twenties and thirties were a very positive time for me both professionally and spiritually. I have loved working in professional theatre for over 20 years, as a theatre manager and organizer of several national festivals, and large-scale projects for children and young people. I travelled throughout India on several occasions during these years, living for a while on ashrams and trekking through the Himalayas, which inspired me to develop my spiritual practice back home in the UK.

While these experiences helped me to develop self-confidence and self-esteem, deep down inside a crippling fear of sexual intimacy and relationships hadn't left me – something inside me felt broken and I couldn't remember why.

For most of my adult life, other than a few vague, fleeting memories, I could not remember anything which happened to me before I was 12 years old. I would look through the family album and see myself on holiday or at a family party, but have no conscious knowledge of being there or of what happened.

Until my early forties, the PTSD effectively served as a powerful anaesthetic in the sense that I had few memories of anything before the abuse took place. It often felt as if the abuse was ALL that had ever happened to me before the age of 12.

The traumatic flashbacks came back with a vengeance several years ago. I was an exhausted workaholic running a theatre, and, while the business was doing incredibly well, I felt completely broken on the inside.

Like many survivors I have met, the main triggers were the horrific revelations that Jimmy Savile had for decades abused so many children and young adults. Every time I saw his vile, smug face I felt an overwhelming rage and I fantasized about hunting Savile down, had he still been alive, and torturing and executing him.

The intensity was terrifying; what could I be capable of doing if I felt the full intensity of this rage? Would my personality fundamentally change to become someone who enjoyed hurting people? Would I become some kind of psychopath?

Yet I knew this wasn't me. I abhor all violence. Suicide seemed to be the most practical option open to me. I can remember on several occasions standing on my third-floor balcony and staring down at the patio beneath me. I was desperately trying to convince myself that there was a swimming pool beneath me and that all I needed to do to kill this horrific mental and emotional agony was to dive head first, so my neck would break and death would be inevitable.

Connecting to immediate professional trauma therapy and crucially with fellow survivors was absolutely vital during this period of my life. The understanding and empathy of fellow survivors is essential for longer-term healing from the trauma of abuse. We just get it...

These aggressive triggers to the abuse were yet another turning point in my life as so many more detailed memories finally came to the surface. I could at last recall the information I needed to heal.

It was not until I could clearly remember the extent of the threats, the menace and the manipulation the paedophiles had used to control me that I was finally able to wholly understand that I really wasn't responsible for what had taken place.

The sense of relief when this happens is immensely healing,

and the emotional freedom is quite literally life changing. The truth is, before the abuse took place, I had a very happy, loving childhood; I just couldn't remember it for so many years, such is the long-term effect of complex PTSD.

It is only more recently that I have been able to write in detail exactly what happened to me during the abuse. With the support of my trauma therapist, I started writing a document which quite naturally evolved during the course of the next 18 months into my memoir: *A Small Boy Smiling*.

There is more of a 'distance' in the memories of the abuse now. I've gradually become more of a 'witness' to the trauma; I can still experience the physical and emotional symptoms, but I am consciously aware that I am a 47-year-old adult remembering what happened during the abuse, rather than being the eight-year-old child reliving the abuse in real-time.

However, sexual intimacy remains an ongoing emotional challenge. A psychologist told me, when I was in my early twenties, that I 'almost had a phobia of relationships'. Looking back, I can see there is much truth in that statement. I was sexually anorexic for many years and until my late thirties even the idea of physical intimacy was a devastating trigger to the abuse. I absolutely dreaded feeling sexually attracted to a woman as it opened up such intense, crippling feelings of sexual inadequacy and self-hatred. It often felt as if the men were standing next to me, threatening and humiliating me.

As a man who has always dreamt of being married and having a family of my own, this reality has been one of the greatest emotional and psychological challenges to come to terms with. However, even in this area of my life I now feel a much greater sense of acceptance and hope.

During the last few years, so much has changed. It has been the years of working the 12-Step Programme, regular meditation, the life-changing support I've received from my loving family, fellow CSA survivors, and the expertise of highly gifted trauma therapists that have helped me to change the inner narrative so that I am able to, for the most part, replace the negative conditioning of the abuse with more gentle, kinder and loving thoughts.

Lucy

As a survivor of childhood sexual abuse, I spend most of my time trying to switch off the negative voice that conditions me to blame myself for anything remotely adverse in life. If I allow it, this voice will relentlessly shout at me, denying me the right to live in the present and experience joy. I have spent thousands of hours in the therapist's chair trying to tame it, but it still catches me unaware at times, most often when I am doing the 'normal' things that 'normal' people do, meeting life milestones, sometimes with a secret but gleeful one finger up to the past.

Before I had any control or reflection on these thoughts, that is before I told anyone about the sexual abuse I experienced as a child, I lurched from crisis to crisis. In a permanent state of denial, I was constantly seeking out negative experiences to reinforce my low self-worth, and finding negativity in most things around me, attempting to hide my own inner pain which I hoped would simply disappear if I ignored it for long enough.

When I finally disclosed, accountability felt important, but three failed police investigations over ten years of my campaigning enabled both the religious figures who sexually abused me to walk free. (I'm not alone – our broken criminal justice system means that 98 per cent of reported sexual assaults do not get a conviction.)

There is a huge grief and loss here, for years that can never be brought back, pain that can never be undone, memories that can never be forgotten. This makes subsequent losses more difficult to bear. Although I did not 'win' and at times the investigation and its blunders felt unbearable, I still found the process invaluable, alongside intensive therapy, in helping me to understand that the abuse was no one's fault but theirs.

I know that my actions since, while not always helpful, were the only response I could give to such a trauma. That because I was abused, it does not mean that I am responsible in any way for others' pain or that only bad things will happen to me. It is very easy to get consumed by 'victimhood', especially during those times that life throws its challenges, as it does to everyone. As children, we believe ourselves to be omnipotent, to have more control over life experiences than we do. The abusers capitalize on this, telling us it is our fault, a belief that becomes cemented into our developing brains.

Suffering is inevitable for all humans but it is very easy for us as survivors of sexual violence to turn these experiences into something that is our fault, and to reinforce the belief the abuser and then the system told us: this is all we are worth.

For me, this again happened most recently during our journey to becoming parents. This is a rite of passage we are a little later to than most, as it has taken time to challenge the idea that I couldn't be a parent or a partner, to believe that I was in fact capable of giving and receiving love and that I would show enough vulnerability and compromise to both my husband and children to make a lifelong relationship work.

Additionally, having been a teacher and knowing the insecurities and damage left on me by the abuse, I did not want to put these onto my children, as I had seen so many parents do without realizing it. I wanted to learn as much as I could about children's emotional development, so I could better support it. Then I wanted to learn as much as I could about the trauma I experienced, so I could better place it in the context of all life challenges, and not bat it away with denial or anger as I had been doing all my life. These quests for knowledge led me to study a Master of Science in Child Psychotherapy – the study of human development and the effects of trauma – which I did alongside the police investigation and campaigning for a national Inquiry into Institutional Child Sexual Abuse (later to be called IICSA). Finally, just as we were ready to think about becoming parents, the police announced that the trial against one of the men who abused me would not be for another year. I knew I could not go through that stress while pregnant; it was not a stress my unborn baby should also carry, so we had to wait again.

When it was finally (almost) the right time, we were lucky that after only three months we fell pregnant, and like any other first-time mum it enveloped me, even though I tried hard not to let it. I would google what size my baby was while in the supermarket (still only a blueberry); I would recheck my dates on the bus, willing time forward to when I could meet my baby, and I would wonder when it was too early to start acquiring baby clothes (it was too early).

I was very sick, but I didn't care – I believed it to be a sign that my hormones and body were responding to new life. I noticed a slight inner niggling fear – 'Stop! Something unusual and uncomfortable is happening to your body again. Is it okay this time?'

And I replied triumphantly, 'Yes, it is! It's wonderful and the baby can take all s/he needs, for this time, I DO consent!'

But then the bleeding started at 11 weeks and I immediately fell down a black hole. They initially called it a 'threatened miscarriage', and only time would tell.

So I was told to wait; to be silent, and to wait some more. Too many times as women, as victims, we have been told this, but I was too scared to argue this time.

I had to go back for several horribly clinical 'internal scans' where a condom-covered camera probe is inserted up your vagina. I was told my dates were wrong, the baby was smaller than it should be. I knew they were not, but no one was listening, not my baby, not my body and not the doctors.

Penetration, cameras, bleeding, cramps, uncertainty, being silenced, total lack of control over my body, lack of accountability and no consent. Put those things together and you are hard pushed to find a more triggering list for female victims of child sexual abuse.

I stayed in bed, literally, for days. Then when I had to get out, I got very drunk, a lot, started smoking again, and friends stopped calling, unsure what to say in the face of another trauma. This self-sabotage was such a familiar response to the other adversities I had experienced, I was angry I was not in control of it. I feebly tried to find some help but there was nothing specific for abuse survivors miscarrying. Once again, our experience is different, but abuse AND miscarriage affects just over a quarter of women, so where are they?

My next pregnancy was tarred with anxiety, hospital visits (I had severe hyperemesis gravidarum, where I couldn't even drink water so had to be hospitalized several times for dehydration) and panic. I do not have even a milligram of understanding of those women who say they enjoy pregnancy. At six months, previous health problems which were attributed to the childhood abuse I suffered caused complications, and I was admitted to hospital. My waters broke early. I knew I would lose the baby or at the least have her very ill with lifelong disabilities, because I trained myself to always expect the worst. They had to deliver her at seven months, but after only two weeks in the special baby unit we could go home. She defied their predictions and she is perfect, I cannot believe how lucky we are – I'm not sure if I ever will.

Eighteen months later, with the biological clock ticking, we try to get her a sibling and I am scared when I get pregnant after only six months of 'trying'. I ask myself the usual questions, how will we cope with two? I get very sick again and end up in hospital for dehydration again.

I go for our 12-week scan.

'Lucy, it's twins,' the doctor says, 'but I'm sorry to tell you the babies are very small – too small for your dates and I can only see one, so this is almost certainly a miscarriage.'

'Thank you,' I tell her, 'I'm due in early March.' Oh My God... EEEKKKK!!! How will we cope with three?!? I am secretly excited. I always wanted a big family. We'll make it work. Mike will be over the moon.

'I don't think you heard me, Lucy. There are no heartbeats, these pregnancies aren't viable.'

I want to ask my husband Mike if I heard this right or if they are playing me once again, but we are in the middle of the global Covid-19 pandemic and he wasn't allowed in.

I am on my own, semi-naked, feet in stirrups trying to listen to the words the doctor is saying and interpret them for the reality they are. I try to catch my breath and call Mike while the doctor goes to get her boss, a senior male consultant who will confirm her diagnosis, but there is no signal in the basement early pregnancy unit of the hospital. I am alone and told to wait in the stirrups until they come back. The only object I can clutch is my useless phone, and I sob. The doctor comes back with her colleague and I immediately apologize through my tear-soaked surgical mask, for what, I'm not sure, but it feels like the right thing to do. Wait, be silent and apologize when something is wrong. This is an ingrained response to a crisis. I can hear glass splinter as the world threatens to fall around me once again.

I must have surgery to empty my uterus, or 'evacuate products from conception' as it is officially called. The six-day wait for this so-called 'elective procedure' is unbearable; it is a missed miscarriage, meaning my body didn't get the memo that there is no baby there to feed. As such, my hormones are still raging and I am still being very sick, in the belief I am still pregnant.

This seems particularly unfair.

This time I decide to take a breath and try and control the experience, practise what I preach. I tell the anaesthetist that I was abused, and I am particularly anxious about general anaesthetics as a result. I explain I hate the countdown to unconsciousness and in the last operation I had a panic attack at this time. Unlike most who fear anaesthesia, it is not the idea I won't wake up that scares me, but what is done to me without my knowledge or consent. I hold back tears as I describe the fear of the doctor inserting medical implements into my vagina while I am unconscious, to remove a baby I don't want removed. He gets it.

When I enter the theatre, they tell me to take my underwear off under my gown. I immediately start sweating. 'No, she won't be doing that today,' he jumps in, telling me to take a seat on the bed, and I feel calmer.

Instead of asking me to count down to unconsciousness

he talks to me about how to get toddlers to sleep – one of my favourite subjects.

The next thing I know, I wake in the recovery room, with new underwear on. The usual sadness and shock and uncomfortableness at the physical symptoms of cramps and bleeding are there, but I am not also consumed by PTSD. I am experiencing something that many, many women do, and this time while the abuse I experienced massively taints it, it will not catastrophize it more than it needs to.

A miscarriage is horrifically sad and unfair and upsetting, with no reason or accountability and this can make it very hard to come to terms with. In the following days, I cry and shout at my husband; I am so consumed by my own loss and physical pain that I am unable to consider his too. I write down what is in my head, and I realize it hurts so much because this is one too many miscarriages; the feeling of loss is so familiar. When I experience it, like listening to a childhood song or familiar sound, it sends me back to the place where everything feels so dark that it will stay that way forever.

This time I won't let it. I marvel at how amazing my daughter is. I remember that even though it doesn't feel it now, time will heal.

I realize that every time I experience a loss, it awakens the previous griefs I have experienced – the grief of the trial where the men who abused me walked free, the grief of a lost childhood. But I am not also dealing with the trauma of a triggering surgical operation too. The anaesthetist, by giving me some control and showing me some understanding without me having to go into detail, did more to help my recovery than he could ever know.

When tackling childhood abuse it is up to all of us – we are all able to make a tiny difference as the doctor did that day – to see survivors as the individuals they are and allow them to control their own response to trauma. I live to see a different world where we no longer fear what we do not understand but ask the simple question: Are you okay? And how can I help?

Samia

It was never going to go well I suppose, with hindsight. My father came from a background of people who had fled persecution and death, and to come to the UK he joined the military before he was out of his teens. By the time of my birth he had changed his name and had become a drug addict. My mother was a child of the war and the trauma of the evacuee system and they lived together in a fantasy world of hope. The day I was brought home from hospital I was nicknamed 'the devil's child' as I was born out of wedlock into a toxic mix of shame and trauma. I was delivered into the arms of my highly religious maternal grandmother, who was living in the front room of my parents 'cramped and damp one-bedroom rented flat. I don't know if my grandmother was unstable before my birth, or whether her religious beliefs drove her to take scissors and cut up every item in the room where I had been left to sleep alongside her. The tale went that everything – curtains, the sofa, family photos – all went under the sharp knife and I was found next day with the scissors embedded in the pillow next to me and with my ear gashed by the impact. My grandmother was taken away in a straitjacket and the name stuck. My mum saw this as my own fault and would constantly remind me of this, until I stopped speaking to her as an adult. As a baby, I never did cry after that; I became a 'good silent baby' ignoring all my needs for food and comfort, just hoping to survive.

Before I could stand, my dad was taking child abuse photos

of me and selling me to the highest bidder for sexual abuse. Any income was good income for him. My mum ignored all this, and my injuries. I didn't reach my milestones, speaking and walking late. I was later told I liked animals and engines and had little interest in people. I remember hallucinating in a basement. I think I was drugged for some kind of abuse and afterwards told that I had fallen down a trapdoor to explain my injuries. I 'fell' a lot and I was told to say I was 'clumsy'. There were two different realities, which I was instructed to narrate and re-tell. I was told that I had eaten a beautiful cooked tea, when I had not been fed at all. I was told not to disclose my injuries or Social Services would take me to an island where adult men would hurt me all day long and everyone would see how bad I was. I had one persona outside which could convince people that everything was fine, if anyone bothered to ask.

I was a solemn child; my mother leant heavily on me as her confidant about money worries and my father's frequent absences. I knew words for worries before I could say a sentence aloud. I look bewildered in my toddler pictures, adrift in a landscape of fear.

My nursery experience began much as my education continued with confusion and disappointment. Taken to playgroup, I immediately fixated on the sandpit, which was full of construction toys. I loved vehicles, I loved engines. I didn't see the blow coming to my face but I felt it connect to my nose and the blood pulse, the boys telling me to 'get away'. Adult hands pulled me back and shunted me away, 'Silly child, you're a girl, you can't play with those, leave the boys alone.' They dumped me with the girls next to the Wendy house and told me to play dolls. I sat there crying silently and my hope of the world engaging with me was largely crushed. A part of me screamed inside silently. I didn't know what a girl was but I already hated being it.

I didn't know what was wrong with my family but I think other parents saw there was something going on. I told a teacher about my experiences, of the strangers hurting my back and body. Somehow my mum convinced the teacher that I had been taken to a play rehearsal and seen some odd actions. I was always confused. People were always telling me that I put up a good front and made attempts at fitting in, but I struggled to focus, had terrifying nightmares and was jumpy and on edge around adults. My teachers decided I was awkward and uncooperative. Some hit out at me when telling me off, others said that the fact I was left-handed was why I couldn't write, but what they really meant was that I was on the devil's path. They made me use my right hand and hit my left hand if I dared to use that instead. None of this helped me settle or learn to write. I have a picture of me I drew when I was aged six. I appear to be on fire, so full of embers and cold, without proper edges to my body, and screaming. No teachers saw this as concerning. But this is probably an accurate image of how I was to feel for the next two and a half decades.

When I was ten, my dad began telling me that it would be a helpful thing if my parents taught me about sex, as it was confusing to learn it in school and better that they showed me. I had a bad feeling that he was already abusing my younger sister. He had stopped touching me that I was conscious of, but would creep into my room at night and I would wake to find him standing over me or with his hand on my body. I froze often and just tried to go somewhere in my head, anywhere really that wasn't there, being that kid in that life. I often felt out of my body and struggled to coordinate as a result. My body was battered black and blue from my mother's outbursts.

WE ARE STILL HERE

I hid these due to the shame of her constantly telling me that I had 'made her' do this. I knew I had the 'devil child' inside me and was the fragile one and I could do nothing right. My teachers made this worse. Because of my injuries, I was stiff and couldn't do the forward rolls and high jumps that the PE teacher demanded. I was shamed and bullied for this and the whole class laughed at me. Afterwards, I became an easy target for bullies who attacked me on the way home and hit me more, taking my school books, emboldened by the teacher's displays.

At home, as I went into secondary school, I would wake from nightmares desperate to use the toilet and, fearful of my father, I would pee into my waste bin and empty it in the morning. My sister saw this and with my mother taunted me for weeks, with both calling me 'piss bucket' and laughing together like hyenas, mocking me for being scared of the dark.

It was then that I discovered my saviour – cooking – via my peers. I loved it and it became my reason to stay alive, my first love and my life buoy. This was coupled with endurance sports. I was fascinated by the fact that cooking seemed to demonstrate that some adults were reasonable, had ethics, were fun and also interested in motorbike engines!

When I became a teen, my dad died from issues linked to his drug use. This wasn't a great improvement as my mother remained filled with hate and unstable. The only thing that lessened were the racist abuse comments that I was 'the Paki's daughter' due to his brown skin, as in my local environment anyone who was brown was viewed through a racist lens. I retreated into cooking as that was the only thing that made sense. To survive, I lived on a diet of stolen early morning milk and raw eggs, left by the milkman conveniently in the path of my pre-dawn runs.

I left school having failed my exams but was accepted at

college. I got on a little better there, able to find creative ways to express myself, and in the background I became involved in the cookery scene and began to work in hospitality linked to it. Again, I failed my exams and ended up leaving the area I was from in an attempt to find work with cookery. I was incredibly lucky to be taken under the wing of some serious chefs who I respected, and finally an adult offered me some support and reasonable life advice. They were busy, though, and I struggled through, living in squats and working two jobs to keep my mind busy while still feeling on fire, disembodied or as if life wasn't real much of the time. I tried to get mental health and housing assistance but was either squatting or living in sublet rooms as I was on the minimum wage. Having no formal tenancy, I was refused any kind of help. I made my own way, running into a slew of older men, who in retrospect I think targeted me, saying they were my friend and then later aggressively wanting sex. I spent a lot of time going home on night buses and had scary instances of being followed and almost raped. I struggled to maintain emotional relationships and to have sex, as I would dissociate and zone out, or not understand what to do. Everything I had experienced was done to me, I had no idea I was supposed to be an active participant until a boyfriend told me I had sex like someone who had been sexually abused, and I needed to move around more.

My life was a chaos of trying to survive in a big city, getting all my happiness from music and trying to avoid thinking of the past or why I felt so strange much of the time. I had no back-up plan and experienced periods of street homelessness which were terrifying; my peers returned to their parents but this was an option I did not have. I could cut away from my body and work a 20-hour day with no problem and this was seen as a positive, although my body began to buckle and my back pain was so bad, sometimes I had to zone out from my body to get through the day.

Eventually, I was more successful in the hospitality scene and sought therapy privately. My first therapist was useless but I didn't understand that at the time. He sat there silent as I tried to explain myself and occasionally condemned me for talking about my issues with interpersonal relationships and told me that I had to get to the bottom of it, but I had no idea what he meant and he didn't elaborate. He made me feel I was doing it wrong. When I said it didn't seem to be working, he said I was giving in and I had to invest more time. It was really unhelpful and almost put me off therapy as it seemed like another type of abuse.

Later I found a lady who was more relational and humanistic. She was great; she was warm, she listened carefully and commented empathically and correctly. She said she could see I had been to hell and come back. I loved her for it but it highlighted the pain of having no parent. I had not felt cared for by an adult before, and it was painful to understand that this was what others had all the time and I did not. Almost all my friends were also estranged from their difficult parents and most had been violently hurt as children. This was a new world of care and consideration by another and it took me a long time to realize that this was probably most people's normal. I slowly told my story and contemplated what my inner child needed to heal and what my body needed to begin to recover. I said my feelings aloud and I began to have some kind of narrative for my life experiences, though I rarely shared them. I was ashamed and remain so on some levels. When I have tried, it's met with disbelief and comments like 'Someone must have noticed', 'That just sounds a bit dramatic' or 'Your mum would never mean to do that deliberately, you should forgive her'.

I watched the rise of the internet replicate swathes of old child pornography images, now back in public circulation, and wondered if pictures of the pre-school me were still around. Was there now a wider swathe of abusers getting their kicks from masturbating over the crime scenes of my pain?

I'm nearly 70 now and have mostly healed the damage that haunts me, only as result of good person-centred therapy. I have never been able to hold down a relationship that didn't become abusive. I have been lost in a weird limbo between the lower underclass core of my youth and feeling excluded from the middle-class world I now find myself in. The main focus of my peers' conversations is their families and children, and I have none. I can't share why, and we have no cultural reference points in common.

I was always terrified of becoming homeless and clung onto safe jobs where I was being ruthlessly exploited, but could pay the mortgage that I had fought and saved to get so late. I feel 'in my body' now there is no screaming inside, but I often feel regret that I have not reached my potential. My body remains wracked with pain. I have an autoimmune disorder that attempts to cripple me and solidify my bones if I don't fight it daily. I ache and I ache. I pay £50 every two weeks for a sport massage so I can stay mobile and work. There is no NHS assistance for this and many medical professionals now highlight the high instance of autoimmune diseases in trauma survivors, a blighted legacy that I can't escape.

I was diagnosed with dyslexia with neurodiversity only when I paid for an assessment myself in my late thirties. I finally wasn't 'stupid' anymore, I had a serious and observable learning issue. I was given helpful medication only when I paid for a private GP and psychiatrist. I only received helpful therapy when I sacrificed half my income to pursue it. I wish my journey had been easier,

I wish society would accept that these things happen in the UK. I wish that professionals, especially teachers, would pick up on the cues that troubled kids show and not taunt them. Watching the experiences of my charges, 20 years my junior, was not comforting as the system let them down in almost the same way.

Society's most vulnerable and the 'underclass' I came from by the fickle hand of fate continues to replicate generational trauma as there are so few avenues out and so little early intervention offered.

Despite post-traumatic stress disorder and dissociation being listed in the clinician's *Diagnostic Statistical Manual* (DSM), there is almost no awareness of it in mental health services. Very few tools are used to test for it and it is not taught or discussed on most psychiatric or counselling trainings. I got myself out, but have never been able to fully reintegrate with society, as result of the taboos and misconceptions around these more extreme experiences. There is no way to un-see the reality of abuse behind a computer screen or a closed door. I will never truly feel safe in the wider world.

Candice

My body was not my own. That night changed the course of my life. Wherever I was headed before that night took a drastic detour and it took a long time to find my path again.

It happened in a small bedroom in the back of the house. I never felt there was enough room to breathe in that flat. The whole place was crammed full of furniture that was made for a much larger home. When my brother and I came to stay, we slept in that back bedroom. Two single beds had been squeezed in this bedroom, there was barely a space between them.

The night it happened was during the school holidays. I

was ten years old. My brother was a few years older. My view of myself, my brother and the world was never the same again after that night.

Both my brother and I had been sent to board full time in an independent preparatory school. What this meant was that I lived at school for three quarters of the year, brought up within an institution.

Our sibling relationship had changed from that point onwards. My relationship with my parents also changed once I was sent away. They were no longer there and suddenly I had to live life without them. I had to grow up quickly.

So, it makes sense that two siblings separated from their parents, and from each other, may well be looking for connection, for love, for attention, for care? It also makes sense that the boundaries in this sibling relationship may have been compromised and, at the very least, need some guidance.

It is not my place to talk about my brother's experience. I cannot be sure what actually happened to him, and that is his story, not mine. But what I will say is, we had to grow up in an institution looked after by people who didn't really know us. The treatment within that first boarding school was at times emotionally, physically and sexually abusive. From the moment I entered boarding school, there was no privacy. Bathing was carried out in front of the other children and we were washed by the matrons while the other girls lined up waiting. I know the boys experienced something similar. As children, we lost our right to have privacy over our bodies the day we stepped into that boarding school.

I know now that many of our experiences are now deemed unacceptable and many practices within schools have changed. But sending a young child away to boarding school still happens in the UK and is considered an acceptable practice by some, but that story is for another time.

That night in that small bedroom changed me. It awoke my sexuality. My first experience of sexual arousal was connected to feelings of fear, confusion, panic, shame, humiliation and guilt. That night, I deepened the separation from myself to protect ME, a separation that had begun a few years earlier living inside an institution. I have since learnt that this is called disassociation, a very useful protective survival mechanism.

That night, I learnt that sexuality is linked with power. That sex is a currency. It taught me that my body is and would become of high interest to the opposite sex. My brother told me that while he was touching me that night. He explained what would happen to my body when I reached puberty. That night also taught me that I should do what I am told to do, what I am 'asked' to do.

That night changed my relationship with my brother and my sexuality. It didn't take long after that night before I started sneaking out of my dormitory window at my boarding school and up the fire escape stairs to go to the boys' dormitory. I started to go regularly to get into bed naked with my brother's best friend. I was 11 years old. This was my first experience of becoming infatuated with a boy and using my body as a way of getting love, attention and validation.

Throughout my teenage years I was confused by my relationship with my brother. By this time, we were living apart in separate boarding schools, but in the holidays, we spent much of the time together.

The first time I had sexual intercourse was with my brother's best friend when I was 14 years old. At age 14, I was drinking alcohol and smoking crack cocaine. I dropped my first acid tab aged 15. I started shoplifting from the age of 15 and I stopped age 17, when I was arrested and cautioned. Around this time, I was arrested for possession of drugs and strip searched by the police.

From my teenage years, I have alcohol and drug-infused memories of being very physically close to my brother. I am unsure to this day if we engaged in any further sexual behaviour during these years, as I have only fleeting, blurred memories. I know I thought about it regularly, which was mixed with feelings of deep disgust, shame and confusion.

My sexual promiscuity really took over from the age of 15 years old. I had had sexual intercourse with over 30 boys and men by the time I was 17 years old. I engaged sexually with many more than that. I am deeply sad as I look back at that lost teenage girl who was desperately looking for love, attention and validation, ultimately trying to find consistency and safety in that love.

What she got, what I got, was a lot of attention but for all the wrong reasons, and the exact opposite of safety. I took myself into extremely unsafe situations. I was not powerful. I was confused and powerless due to my desperate need to be wanted.

During a family holiday, while at a college house party, I was sexually violated. On the second night of the holiday, my brother told me that he was being asked by the young men he was meeting to set them up with his sister. What I remember from that holiday was getting wasted each night and engaging in some form of sexual act with a stranger I had met that day. I didn't care about my safety, all I needed was to be wanted. I had gone to that house with my brother; it had been full of college-aged men. I had blacked out quickly, whether I was drugged I will never know, but when I came to, in a bed, I knew

WE ARE STILL HERE

I had been sexually violated. I was a teenager, still a child in the eyes of the law. Somewhere in that house was also my brother.

During my early teenage years, I followed my brother into many unsafe situations. I do not blame him for what happened to me. They were my actions. But my brother didn't help me to stay safe – he actually helped me to be unsafe. In a healthy sibling relationship, an older brother would want their sister to be safe. But my brother never valued himself enough to even keep himself safe.

When I was a young adult I visited my brother after he had been released from hospital. I spent the night at his house. There was only one bedroom and one bed. I remember pushing myself to the edge of the bed, not wanting to touch him. Yet at the same time, part of me was fantasizing that we could move to another country and be together. These thoughts would come in, I would become highly aroused and then immediately I would feel disgusted and ashamed. This would lead to suicidal thinking as I felt so trapped within all of this confusion. This had been churning inside me for over ten years.

A few years after the hospital admission, I broke off contact with my brother. He used to phone me, intoxicated and while hurting himself. I had become his caretaker. It was a deeply unhealthy and co-dependent relationship. It was during one of these phone calls that I realized I wasn't looking after myself and in actual fact I wasn't helping him. He didn't listen to anything I said, and, if anything, I was enabling him.

As I write this, I am shocked at how long this destructive and confused relationship continued in this way. I rarely see my brother now. When I am near him now, I feel very uncomfortable and nauseous.

As an adult, I read books on abuse. They stated that the person needed to be at least four years older than the other person

86

for it to be classed as abuse. In the *Diagnostic and Statistical Manual of Mental Disorders*, it states that the person needs to be five years older than the other.

This supported me to continue to push down my feelings and experiences. It enabled me to continue to be confused and blame myself for what had happened to me when I was ten years old.

But I remember that night. My brother had spoken to me with an authority, telling me about how my body would change when I hit puberty. I felt exposed. I was laid out, on show. It was not an innocent game on his part. When he touched me and put his fingers inside me, he knew what he was doing and what he wanted when he showed me what to do to him. I remember not wanting to touch him. I was frightened. I was so embarrassed. But I did what he told me to do because I felt I had to.

I felt like a bad person. Throughout the whole experience, we could have been exposed. I was on high alert and panicked. At some point, I found my strength and stopped what I was doing to him, jumped into my bed and put my head under my covers. He was annoyed at me but then carried on. He masturbated until he ejaculated. I didn't know what was happening. This was my first experience of any sexual contact.

I felt so guilty for not carrying on as I felt I was 'meant to'. Another part of me wanted all this to stop, for me to disappear from the situation. I wanted to feel safe again. We had to share that bedroom for the rest of the half-term break. He continued to masturbate each night with me in the bed next to him. I dreaded the night-times.

How did this affect me? Carrying a burning shameful secret inside me fuelled a pattern of harmful sexual behaviours throughout my teenage years and embedded a deep self-loathing. I was raped and sexually assaulted a number of times during these years. Back then, I did not believe I had the right to say 'No', and when I did, I was not listened to.

In my early thirties, I tried to speak to someone, who seemed like an appropriate person in a position of trust and authority. It took a long time for me to get the first words out, which said something about when I was young there was sexual behaviour that happened between me and my brother and that I felt unsure about it. Almost immediately, they responded with: 'Do not make this into something bigger than it was, sexual experimentation happens between siblings.'

The impact of their response on me was huge. The speed at which they responded, along with what they said, was so dismissive.

I had been shut down. I had wanted to share about an incident that had plagued my mind for the past 20 years, to talk about the feelings that I had carried since then – the shame, guilt and confusion. I felt dismissed. It was confirmed to me that what I had been telling myself all these years – that I was 'making things up', 'making them into something bigger than they were' – was all true. I should listen to the voice that had been telling me for years to 'shut the fuck up and forget about it'.

Well, I had been trying, hadn't I, for 18 years? And it hadn't worked.

I still feel like this when I talk to my current therapist about these events, even though she has never once dismissed or judged me. I am still trying to allow my feelings to surface, to accept what happened, the harm that has been done to me. I want to be able to release it. I want to move on from it, to stop it plaguing my mind.

I was not there to make my brother the 'bad one'. I am still not wanting to make my brother the 'bad one'. What I have learnt is that I was a victim and my brother was both a perpetrator and a victim himself.

This professional person had been there to teach me. They certainly taught me what not to do, the perfect example of how to shut someone down, how to misuse your power and reinforce abusive patterns of behaviour. They acted without consideration or care for me.

I never challenged them at the time. I felt disempowered and that they were in control. I was too frightened to challenge them. Years later, I did go back and say what I needed to say. I was heard but they did not apologize to me for what had been said. I knew they still had not learnt anything about sibling abuse, but at that point, neither had I.

Who was this professional to make such blanket statements to me? When I sat in front of them, clearly struggling, upset and confused and they heard ONE sentence – the only words I could manage to get out – what gave them the right to dismiss my experience and dismiss ME in the process?

Because of this, I didn't get to speak about what actually happened that night and the impact that one event had on me. Not only that, but I didn't get to talk about the resulting unhealthy, destructive relationship that formed between me and my brother, or the addictive and damaging acting-out behaviour that began and continued throughout my life.

None of this did I speak about with them, the trained professional. None of this did I get the chance to bring out of the dark, to stop burying, to bring clarity to, to understand, to forgive myself and others, to release, to move on.

So yes, I was angry, angry even more than I was before.

I was even more angry with myself – for opening up when I KNEW it wasn't safe to talk about. I was angry that I took a risk to trust someone to hear me. And that I did that again. Twice. Two professionals dismissed my experience – dismissed me.

The second time, over five years after the first, I opened up and decided to talk to another professional. Again, a similar experience. After only one sentence had been uttered, an immediate response: 'These things happen between brother and sister.'

This time I had enough courage to contact them afterwards and challenge them on it. This time, I am grateful to say this person was incredibly apologetic. Their words were: 'I am so sorry, I don't know why I said that.'

We are all human, so we all make mistakes. I know I have as a counsellor and it is incredibly painful when you realize you have inadvertently hurt someone. But we need to learn from our mistakes to ensure that we do not do it again. We need to understand why what we did was a mistake.

I accepted their apology but decided to end our working relationship. I finally felt empowered for standing up for myself. I had defended my little girl at long last.

I have spent a lifetime dismissing myself. What this meant was that I had turned the anger in on myself. This reinforced my belief that I didn't deserve to be listened to, that my needs didn't matter, that I was not deserving of love and attention. I didn't need a professional to dismiss me too.

So, as is the way, these feelings went underground and showed up in my life in destructive and addictive behaviour. For me, this was most obvious in my sexual behaviour and my partner relationships. I desperately tried to manipulate situations and others so that I was loved and wanted but all that did was create the opposite.

It is only in the last three years that I have found therapists who have really listened and heard my experience without judging or dismissing me. I am now in my mid-forties. I deeply value these professionals whom I have worked with, each for differing reasons. None of them has shut me down. None of them has dismissed me.

And it is with my current therapist that I have finally got to truly understand the dynamics of sibling sexual abuse. I am finally starting to truly acknowledge the harm that was done to me by my brother and at the same time recognize he was also a victim.

It was such a breakthrough moment for me to be finally seen and my experience to be acknowledged at long last. My brother, only a few years older than me, was a perpetrator of abuse, he had power over me with his level of knowledge and the stage of his sexuality. He knew what he wanted when he engaged me in the behaviour that night. He took control of the situation for his own benefit. I did not know what I was 'agreeing' to.

I still need to be careful when I am around my brother, otherwise he will try to reconnect with me. But I know that this is not healthy for me and it is not emotionally safe. My brother and I have never spoken about the abuse or our resulting unhealthy, destructive relationship. All the secrecy and shame. I am afraid that he is too unstable to be able to hear it. I know I am caretaking again, but I do not wish my brother any harm. I am also aware that I am only just beginning to come to terms with everything that happened between us.

Alastair

The abuse started when I was about four, and carried on intermittently until I was about 11. My abuser groomed me in such a way that I was left feeling completely responsible for what went on. He pretended to be asleep, so that I thought I was doing things to him without him knowing. With therapeutic hindsight, I understand now that he'd orchestrated the whole thing, slowly seducing me into performing sexual acts with a game about sucking thumbs. On the last occasion that it took place, he told me that I was 'a very naughty boy', and that he'd tell my mum. He was really someone I admired, I thought he was my friend, and at the time of the abuse I thought we were playing some sort of game. I didn't think what was happening was bad until he said that.

I did not disclose the abuse until I was 18, and in the intervening years I tried to make sense of what had happened, what kind of person I was and was going to become given that as a child I had done those things to a sleeping old man. I had heard about abuse as something that adults did to children, but the only way that I could rationalize my specific experiences was to assume responsibility, to see myself in the abusive role.

As a teenager, I compulsively worried about all this and thought it meant that I was fundamentally bad and sexually perverted. It's clever really; by making me believe it was my fault he ensured that I wouldn't be able to talk about what happened for a long time, because I was so ashamed of it and scared that I'd done something really bad. I now know that the shame, which has become completely infused into my sense of self, should have been his alone to bear. I think the teenage years of trying to rationalize the abuse have been as damaging as the abuse itself, because it was during this time that I formed a very distorted picture of myself that became deeply ingrained and subsequently affected my adult relationships and sense of myself in the world.

The girlfriend who I first told about the abuse was really

supportive and loving but hardly equipped to help me properly understand what had happened. At that stage, I was still pretty confused about the abuse, trying to absolve the abuser of responsibility, because there were many things I had valued about spending time with him, not least the companionship. After seeing a counsellor for a short stint on the encouragement of my girlfriend, I did at least begin to intellectually understand that it was his responsibility to have stopped that from happening, that kids are sexually curious and that's normal, and that adults in charge of those kids shouldn't exploit that. I think it was a big relief to hear this but it didn't really scratch the surface of how damaging the abuse really was to my sense of self.

When I told my mum about what had happened a couple of years later, she tried to minimize my experiences, focusing on the actual physical content of the abuse and expressing relief that I hadn't been raped or physically hurt (I had, in fact, sustained an injury, but I didn't share that). In fairness, I think I hadn't really grasped the full impact that the abuse had had on me at this time, and I was still minimizing it. It was something that I thought I should be able to deal with. My mum told some of my siblings about what had happened, and while one was and has continued to be relatively supportive, the other one tried to minimize what had happened to me, and really discouraged me from dwelling on it and told me to move on, to rise above it. The implication was that the abuse could be a weakness or a strength, and it was up to me to choose which it was to be. Unfortunately, I took heed of this advice and tried to be positive and strong. I wish someone around me at that time had understood that any abuse can have really serious impact for the victims and had encouraged me to seek proper psychotherapeutic help.

In my early twenties, I tried to get on with life like my friends were doing, and had a lot of fun. I look back fondly on aspects of those years. But in many respects, I felt hampered. I had very low self-esteem, little confidence in myself, and felt depressed and hopeless a lot of the time. I was always shy, but managed to enjoy socializing with the help of alcohol. At university, I developed a serious anxiety about talking in groups, and developed such a phobia of doing so that I repeatedly failed to turn up to seminars. This anxiety in groups is something that I struggle with to this day. Despite my academic degree, I felt that any 'white-collar' job would be beyond me because it would undoubtedly involve this kind of interaction with groups. Thus I sought work where I was safe from this kind of exposure. For a lot of my twenties I wrote music and played in bands and put a lot of hope in this being successful. I never quite had the courage to see anything through, or get my songs finished to a point where I was brave enough to perform them. I started working as a gardener, which has become my occupation and something that I love. As well as it being pretty reliably free from public-speaking opportunities, I am sure that working outdoors and with my body has nourished what little confidence I had in myself, and has been a real source of strength for me. I also worked in second-hand bookshops, which were an intellectually stimulating environment but also a very non-judgemental one, populated with people, customers and staff who were often unconventional to say the least. These were safe spaces in which to engage with others, where there was never any judgement.

Through my twenties, I struggled to engage with sex in a healthy way. The culture among my peers was a licentious one that I attempted to partake of. I felt a huge amount of anxiety around dating, and could only really feel brave enough to talk to women after a lot of alcohol. I had plenty of one-night stands but without exception they were drunken encounters, and any sex was initiated and proceeded in a cloud of inebriation. I can now see that underneath that shield of alcohol I was extremely vulnerable during many of those encounters, that sex and being fully in my body was actually a very risky, triggering thing for me, and that all the time I was struggling to shake this sense of myself as somehow sexually bad and perverse.

I did have more serious relationships but I was mostly a nervous wreck during these, besotted with the other person and desperate for them to love me and approve of me, though I could never trust them or believe I was worthy of their love. It was impossible for me to achieve this and my failure to do so was evidence to my judgemental inner voice that I was worthless, hopeless and bad at heart. I think this need for approval meant I was often not able to leave relationships when I was suffering or not being respected. More often than not I would resist anything getting serious; if it looked like it might then I would drop the thing – 'ghosting' is the expression used now – and really hurt people just by not being able to communicate. Often what I thought was waning interest on my part was really terror about the possibility of having to be vulnerable with someone and put myself at risk of rejection. At the same time, I felt awful about my behaviour, that I was behaving disrespectfully and unkindly to people.

In my mid-twenties, child sexual abuse started getting a much higher profile in the media, particularly in relation to Jimmy Savile. Simultaneously, there seemed to be more and more discussion in the press about the issue of sexual consent in general. All this must have been quite triggering for me. I had a lot of feelings pushing up to do with my own abuse that I didn't really know how to deal with. At the same time, I started to obsessively scrutinize all my past sexual encounters, worrying that I had crossed boundaries with people, or worse, that I might have assaulted people. I was really in pieces about this; I feared that I had become an abuser. These obsessive moralizing ruminations were paralysing and I began to find functioning normally very difficult. I felt I couldn't talk to anyone because anyone I shared these worries with would be disgusted by me. It was just the same as the anxieties I'd had as a teenager about what had happened with the abuser; again, I was burdened with a terrible secret.

Eventually, I managed to muster the courage to ask for help. I knew that all the Jimmy Savile stuff was stirring up feelings and bringing my childhood abuse to the front of my mind; but I also was desperate for someone to help me not to judge my own behaviour in my past sexual encounters.

I found a therapist who specialized in child sexual abuse and have now been seeing her for over eight years. Little did I know how much I needed this professional support. I was able to disclose everything fully, and explore all of my fears about whether I had behaved inappropriately with sexual partners in the past. I now feel confident that I have not been abusive to anyone else. I also understand that these fears about my behaviour as a young adult stemmed from the false belief, instilled at the time of my own childhood abuse, that I was responsible for what was taking place and therefore was the perpetrator. I can see that the need to judge myself, and the rumination which I have been tormented by – about every thought I have, or everything that I have done or might do – is the legacy of that period of time as a teenager when I was trying to make sense of what I had experienced when I was little. A consequence of undertaking to write this account has been that I have felt the courage to share all of this with my current partner, which feels like a huge achievement after so many years feeling shame. This means I can feel wholly loved, and although the patterns of rumination are still intrusive and sometimes debilitating, I feel very supported in enduring them when they arise.

PRACTITIONERS

Maria

I work therapeutically with both men and women survivors of CSA. I help them find a greater sense of safety and security and start on the road to recovery with growth from trauma, resilience and understanding how to manage trauma symptoms.

I have gained extensive experience in CSA, domestic violence, narcissist abuse, rape and trauma-related experiences. I have developed a training programme on PTSD which I deliver to the emergency department of a hospital, GP surgeries, eating disorder units, the police and local councils. I worked for a charity for four and a half years, then went on to support survivors for a well-known project. I currently work as a private practitioner.

The effects of CSA can leave a person with debilitating and consuming symptoms of CPTSD or PTSD. Learned coping mechanisms from childhood trauma can be confusing.

There are many important aspects of this work. Making them feel believed is paramount. Giving them a voice, allowing them to be heard without being shamed and really being there for the survivor wherever they are on the journey of healing feels important. Equally important, I feel, is not to rush the process of healing – limitations of timings can feel overwhelming and unhelpful. I remember someone saying as a survivor that "'you have six sessions" felt like a green light was on, but the red light was too close'.

It is vital to help a survivor feel safe in their world, creating a real, trusting place where they can learn to trust in themselves and others. I keep it real and work with relational depth in my work, speaking in layman's terms while we work together to facilitate change.

The subject is close to my heart; I have always felt humbled to be in a place to help survivors. To be able to facilitate the survivor's journey of healing is what makes my job worthwhile. The process of healing can be painful at times, but working through the pain leads a survivor to a place of empowerment, growth and resilience, diminishing feelings of self-sabotage, guilt and shame. It changes feelings of helplessness, worthlessness and powerlessness, ingrained for many years, to feelings of confidence and inner strength.

Self-care and stabilization are a large part of the work I offer survivors, including understanding triggers and learning new ways to manage emotional and physical flashbacks. There are no 'on and off' buttons for trauma symptoms, so I help the survivor to learn ways to understand and manage them, almost turning the volume down. Identifying triggers is an important part of prevention to avoid relapsing into self-medicating and self-harm. Triggers can be difficult reminders of past traumatic experiences, leaving a person feeling unsafe and potentially heightening trauma symptoms. Triggers can cause a survivor to have flashbacks. Flashback and emotional flashback management can be helpful to a survivor. Triggers can often be activated by sensory stimuli. During trauma, sensory stimuli are stored in the brain. Association of triggers with the trauma needs to be unpicked and understood. It is impossible to avoid triggers, but knowing how to prepare for and manage them through the processing of feelings related to the traumatic events, learning grounding techniques or re-learning healthy behaviours to manage this uncomfortable distressing time can be helpful. Know your triggers.

The process of healing takes time and patience and I help survivors to manage their expectations and reflect that this journey can be painful at times but eventually empowering.

Within my work, I incorporate trauma-informed psychoeducation. It feels important to help the survivors understand their trauma symptoms without shaming the aftermath of such violations. I work with dissociation (which can present as depression), understanding times of hypervigilance, recognizing avoidance, numbing of trauma reminders and re-experiencing.

Quite often in my work, dissociation or 'checking out' can manifest in different ways. The mind learns how to escape the body and this becomes a coping strategy, the brain telling us that we can carry on with a 'normal life' as dissociation protects us from overwhelming feelings. I feel it's important not to shame this clever coping mechanism, used at times to push painful memories away for some survivors for many years. Dissociative amnesia can hold the traumatic memories away, but when the memories flood back at any time in a survivor's life, this can be frightening and confusing. Some memories can be fragmented, which can feel frustrating for some survivors. Working with dissociation and the fragmented memories can be helpful for a survivor and less shaming if a diagnosis of dissociate disorders has been given – let's face it, the word 'disorder' can make a survivor feel more shame.

I help survivors to learn new coping mechanisms to manage

WE ARE STILL HERE

intense feelings of distress when remembering CSA and understand how this might impact physically on the body. If they learn how to be aware, they can then manage any symptoms.

Another issue is victim blaming and shame. Often survivors internalize feelings of 'why didn't I run or fight back or scream?' It feels important to psychoeducate them the impact on the brain's amygdala and hippocampus. The job of the amygdala, the external alarm bell, is to keep us all safe, picking up vibes from our senses and its super-fast reaction when it spots potential danger, getting the body ready to flight, fight, freeze and, for some in cases of abuse, 'friend'. It is fast and automatic, meaning it is good for the job. A survivor may not have been able to run or fight back, and the shame attached to not being able to defend themselves from psychological kidnap brings up many frustrations, so it can be useful to remind the survivor that it's not them who decides how to respond to fear, it's the amygdala. Survivors often ask why they experience similar feelings when remembering a traumatic memory, so it can help to explain the role of the hippocampus, the brain's filing cabinet, and how the 'normal' memories are stored differently from trauma memories. Trauma memories are not tagged with a time and a place like a normal memory, so when those memories are remembered it can feel for a survivor as if it's happening again, and the feelings and thoughts can be intense. By understanding these brain functions and knowing when the amygdala is ringing off the hook, survivors can work to get back to a stable place when triggered.

Thinking about shame and understanding trauma bonds, one of the most difficult attachments to break, can also be helpful in coming to terms with understanding attachments to some abusers. Love and fear chemicals are stronger than healthy love bonds. The imbalance of power and reward can be confusing for some survivors, who may find it difficult to break this attachment. Understanding the power of a trauma bond and the punishment/reward relationship can be freeing for some survivors.

Helping the survivor to identify triggers and finding ways to manage them and correlate the emotions attached to them, recognizing patterns and response and improving awareness by using grounding techniques and self-care has been useful within my work.

Another common thread in my work is that a survivor may feel as if they are 'going mad'. Not understanding trauma symptoms and not being helped to understand their feelings might lead to an overwhelming sense of fear and confusion. Difficult symptoms can include intrusive thoughts, shame, guilt, nightmares, flashbacks, anger, tricky relationships with food, communication problems, concentration difficulties, feeling on edge, insomnia and not knowing who to trust. Experiences like smear tests, childbirth, visits to the GP, dentist or hospital settings can be re-traumatizing for a survivor. This thread appears often in my work. The combination of CSA and the perpetrator being in control of the survivor's body then going into what some may feel as a normal experience can be extremely upsetting for a survivor, at times taking them to a place of re-traumatization.

It is important to understand that, for some survivors, asking them to forgive and accept the abuser is not always appropriate. Forgiving someone who has almost destroyed the survivor's sense of safety and made their world unsafe for many years is not okay.

This subject is forever a place of learning. I am helping survivors to reach a place of stabilization, resilience and understanding, and enabling them to safely process childhood sexual abuse. I thank survivors for trusting in me to walk beside them while they heal.

Reena

I write this in the midst of a swelling growth of the Black Lives Matter movement. As I've been engaging with this particular incarnation of the movement, and the growing global consciousness of the legacy of slavery and colonialism, I have been struck by the intersection between the shame I carried in relation to my abuse history and the internalized racism I have held about the race, culture and community I grew up in.

My abuse took place within my family home where, like many South Asians who arrived as refugees from Uganda, I lived in an extended family set-up. I grew up being forever reminded both by the world around me, and by my mother, that my experience was 'other'. The norm was the white English experience where people lived within a nuclear family, those indigenous to the mother country. Both my parents were raised as subjects of the British Empire in India and Kenya. They fully swallowed the belief that white people are superior and they passed this belief on to me. However, my mother was at great pains to try to keep the culture alive in us, ensuring that I learned to read and write Gujarati at the same time as I was learning English. There were confusing messages in this upbringing – our culture is something to be proud of and something to hold on to, but we should respect the superiority of the culture and the ways of the mother country.

In my childhood mind, when I carried the shame of my abuse experience, I believed it to be something that could only occur in Asian households. I conflated aspects of my cultural upbringing to make some logic of this. Sex was not openly discussed and sexuality was to be hidden: surely this was why young men would perpetrate the abuse as they had no healthy, natural outlet. Women's sexuality was particularly problematic. Pre-pubescent girls were considered pure and would be revered in religious gatherings; menstruation, on the other hand, was unclean and girls and women were not allowed near religious shrines or in temples if they had their period. I was confused by this belief system and struggled, not least because I believed I wasn't pure as a pre-pubescent child, taking full responsibility for the clandestine encounters at night, which I learned much later were 'abuse'.

The abuse ended when I was ten years old, and as an adolescent I grew to make more sense of the world around me. As I did so, I grew to have a disdain for the naive, limited and misogynistic way of thinking within my cultural and religious upbringing. I saw the beliefs and practices as wholly serving the males within the community, while keeping the women downtrodden.

While I had somewhat split off the details of the abuse and the corollary shame, I gravitated as a young adult towards structures which held structural and cultural capital. Through my hunger for high art (English literature, European fine art, Western classical music and jazz), I was white-washing myself – in my mind it was a kind of purification. The more immersed I became in this Western, English world, the more I endeavoured to keep the abuse locked away and hidden – it was not me. I became ever more integrated in the Western culture around me, adopting the accent which could afford me access to other worlds, having few Asian friends, and believing that I was going up in the world.

One feature of having a history of chronic abuse, which was kept secret from all, was the way in which I developed a facility

WE ARE STILL HERE

to read the environment around me, and mould myself to meet the other's needs. I had learned, unconsciously, to put my own needs to one side in the service of the other; and I had learned, unconsciously, how to offer up different versions of myself depending on what was called on by the environment around me: I became a chameleon. But the chameleon lizard has the capacity to change its colour. Whatever internal white-washing I undertook, I forgot that I did not change colour – what people encounter first and foremost when they meet me is my brown skin. I wonder now if some of the labour I undertook to blend in with the white cultures was a vain attempt to rid myself of the stain of my abuse.

Power and child sexual abuse

I believe that a great deal of my disavowal of my Asian heritage was an attempt to reclaim some personal power, in the wake of the powerlessness of the abuse. Given that I am from an ethnic minority, I now see that much of my villainizing of men and the patriarchy within South Asian culture was also influenced by the media's portrayal. In recent years, the media portrayals of the grooming gangs and child sexual exploitation in Rotherham and other locations served to reinforce stereotypes, in particular of Muslim men and men of Pakistani heritage, but also of South Asian men more broadly, as dangerous, criminally minded, and backward.

In 2011, the former home secretary Jack Straw stated:

there is a specific problem which involves Pakistani heritage men…who target vulnerable young white girls… We need to get the Pakistani community to think…about the problems that are leading to a number of Pakistani heritage men thinking it is OK to target white girls in this way... So they then seek other avenues and they see these young women, white girls who are vulnerable, some of them in care...who they think are easy meat. (Batty, 2011)

When living in a community where there are a range of people from the same ethnicity and culture, one can see that some people may be difficult while many others are good-hearted: there is an openness to recognize a broad range of characters. Conversely, there can be a tendency to be reductive and thin the characteristics to be attributed to an ethnic minority so that people will, unconsciously or semi-consciously, ascribe a propensity for sexual exploitation tendencies towards men of South Asian heritage. I believe that these views within the media at large solidified my personal wariness of South Asian men. What I wasn't able to consider until more recently was the possibility that the overpowering of vulnerable young girls (white or brown) might itself be a patriarchal response to a wider structural disempowerment.

Structural and systemic power

As I write about the way my experience played into tropes of South Asian men, I notice a discomfort that I too am reinforcing these narrow, reduced stereotypes. I think of Crenshaw's seminal thinking on intersectionality. When describing how data was suppressed about battered women of colour, she stated there was a concern that:

the data would unfairly represent African-American and Latino communities as unusually violent, potentially reinforcing stereotypes that might be used to justify oppressive police tactics and other discriminatory practices. These misgivings are based on the familiar and not unfounded premise that certain minorities – particularly Black men – have already been stereotyped as pathologically violent. (Crenshaw, 1994, pp.97–98)

This fear of feeding negative stereotypes about the minority communities where the abuse has occurred often serves to silence further our experience of being victims of abuse. At the same time, if we don't try to remain open to the transgenerational roots behind abuse, and focus only on the specific experience of the victim/survivor, there is a risk that we may inadvertently collude with, and reinforce, these tropes.

In my work with survivors of colour, I have been struck by the systemic quality of the abuse: abuse rarely occurs in a vacuum, and the perpetrator has often also been a victim. What I notice is that there is always a great deal of trauma within the family systems, and that even if the perpetrator's abuse history is not known, there has often been developmental and relational trauma. The perpetration of abuse then is a broken and damaged way of exerting power in the face of the powerlessness which the perpetrator has felt for much of their life. When we look at experiences of abuse among people of colour in the UK, we cannot ignore the legacy of the transatlantic slave trade and colonialism. Menakem, writing of racialized trauma, states: 'Most of us think of trauma as something that occurs in an individual body, like a toothache or a broken arm. But trauma also routinely spreads between bodies, like a contagious disease' (Menakem, 2017, p.37). He describes the perpetration of abuse as a way of trying to soothe their own trauma, choosing 'dirty pain over clean pain...by blowing it through another person – using violence, rage, coercion, deception, betrayal, or emotional abuse' (Menakem, 2017, p.37). The language of dirty pain and clean pain is powerful, illustrating how trauma, pain and abuse are perpetuated if the intergenerational cycle is not broken. The cycle can only be broken by sitting with the pain, bearing the pain, growing the capacity to tolerate the pain, rather than blowing it through another body.

When working with my clients of colour who are survivors, there is a risk that I inadvertently collude with white supremacy (Saad, 2020) by only focusing on the villainy of the perpetrator of my client's sexual abuse. It seems important to recognize that much of the patriarchal violence, enacted within communities from colonized countries, may itself be a trauma response (choosing dirty pain) stemming from the subjugation and emasculation of black-skinned and brown-skinned men at the hands of white slave masters and colonizers. In addition to this emasculation, the maltreatment of black-skinned and brown-skinned women at the hands of white men was rife, and one can see how a hierarchy can be internalized which supports patriarchy – a man of colour can believe he has some power by subjugating a girl or a woman, even when he has none in relation to the white power structures he is subservient to.

While I am in no way trying to excuse the abusers' actions or be an apologist for them, I feel that not using this wider societal lens could result in a further promotion of dirty pain. I believe that the work that my clients do, by coming to therapy to work with their history of abuse, is a counter-cultural effort to develop the capacity to soothe their trauma through the clean pain, and thus break the intergenerational cycle of trauma. However, one of the strongest characteristics of being a survivor, which I recognize in my own experience, is a hatred of the powerlessness which was inherent in the experience of the abuse. Within the work, a great deal of focus can be on how to overcome this sense of powerlessness and regain a sense of power and control – moving from victim to survivor. This is often achieved through a rebalancing of the power dynamic between perpetrator and victim, feeling one's own power and deriding and denigrating the perpetrator. The survivor may choose legal redress as a way of reclaiming their power – it is something I have often considered. Yet my struggle with this route is that it makes the ordeal too binary – there is insufficient recognition that we were all victims of trauma. And there is a danger that the dirty pain is blown through another body as a way of expelling it from our nervous system. The work of healing therefore needs to be a broader, more nuanced project: being able to hold the paradoxes and contradictions, and the wider historical context, in order to support survivors' capacity to bear our trauma, hold our clean pain and settle the dysregulation in our bodies.

Jane

When a client has the courage to share their experience of childhood sexual abuse I have my own internal response, which has always included sadness and anger for what the client has experienced. My response is an important guide as survivors of sexual abuse may not be able to have these feelings for themselves in their survivor position.

Childhood sexual abuse is a violation of trust and of boundaries. Part of surviving is forming an internal boundary, which may mean a client not allowing themselves to feel anything, not trusting themselves in intimacy, and staying hidden. As a therapist, I need to be sensitive and appreciative of where a client begins their therapy with me.

Only the client can know their experience of the abuse and the impact that the abuse has had on them. I'm a curious therapist and I ask clients to find their curiosity too, to become aware of themselves, their experiences and their internal responses.

Their responses to the abuse are all valid and needed to manage the abuse and its impact on them. I'm interested in how these responses, which served the client then, may not be serving them so well now, and how a client can form something different.

For example, I am curious about how a client responds to their anger and how they might express it or internalize it.

Survivors of childhood sexual abuse are the victims of perpetrators who are angry and aggressive. A direct consequence on a survivor may be for them to be afraid of any anger, including their own. Their own anger can be internalized, and they may never express their frustration or needs for fear of an aggressive response from others. That is when their history is playing out in the now.

I work with clients to help them to get to know their feeling of anger and for them to not be afraid of it; to be able to listen to it and express it in a safe and level way. When we aren't afraid of our own anger we will be less afraid of others' anger.

For some survivors, to have found their rage at the time of the abuse could have been life threatening, enraging the perpetrator more, so the survivor instinct is to keep quiet – a necessary and important response at the time.

Going forward into adulthood, imagine that response now remains a part of the way you form yourself. How you might speak to yourself – I can't tell that person no or say 'I don't want that' or 'I don't want to do that' because they will just get angry. So you stay silent and say you are fine.

You leave yourself out of the conversation, as in that moment you are still in survival mode.

What if you didn't need to be in survival mode for that moment? How could you respond differently and in a way where you are an integral part of the conversation?

For some clients, this concept is a revelation and I'm often asked, 'Can I do that?' Sadly I'm more often told, 'I'm not doing that, it's not worth it.' To both these responses I feel sad because this is the legacy of their abuse. I also feel optimistic because we have started a new conversation.

I might start by asking a client to notice when they stop themselves responding to their needs; saying 'yes that's fine' when internally there is either a 'no' or a 'not sure' or 'nothing'. My aim is to help the client become more aware of their needs and, importantly at this stage, how they don't respond to their needs.

We start to notice a pattern of appearing fine when the client is far from fine. This takes effort from the client because I am asking them to notice themselves. When the survival pattern is to stay silent and hidden, then I am asking a lot of them to find their voice. It takes courage from the client and trust in me and themselves. There is no rush or expectation from me on the right or wrong way of doing this.

I am mindful of the importance for a survivor to experience a considered, empathetic and kind therapist. That doesn't mean I just tilt my head and patronize the client. They deserve more, they deserve my effort and they deserve authenticity and integrity. Survivors of childhood sexual abuse are courageous and, in my experience, they want a robust therapist.

When a client develops their self-awareness, they start

to have a choice of responding differently. This is far from the options available as a child being abused. The difference is that this is now and not then. When it feels like then, the survivor instinct comes into play. However, in the now, when the client has more awareness they can experience themselves, not as the child, but as an adult who has a voice and can define themselves differently.

Let me use what might seem a simple example but holds the complexity of the survival instinct. You have a friend who you really like and is kind and caring and fun and all things you want in a friend. Whenever you arrange to meet up, this friend is always late and not just by five minutes because of unavoidable delays but late late, 30 minutes plus late. Every time, you wait patiently because you like spending time with them and they always show up eventually. So you say it's fine for you to wait and for the friend to be late. How much of that is the survivor in you? What if it was okay to say to the friend, 'I want you to be on time when we arrange to meet up'? A client will have a response to that ranging from fear to excitement. This is a good friend they are talking to, so a good person to practise on. It can be a small step to say something and it is also a giant leap. Saying something doesn't mean the friend will never be late again, that isn't the point of the exercise. The point is for the client to know that they have needs and deserve respect and to hear themselves say, 'This is me and I have needs.' This is the client saying 'no', in a respectful way, to a friend's pattern of behaviour that doesn't work for the client.

Through the therapy, I ask clients to respond to themselves as a way of helping them to not react to the legacy of their abuse. A survivor of sexual abuse knows how to react, they know how to keep themselves internally 'safe'. Their body may tighten and freeze, they may have feelings of shame and fear and dissociate to separate themselves from the abuse and the memory re-experiencing of the abuse. I don't want a client to ever lose that instinct. They needed it then and at times they need it now. What I do want to encourage is a client to have alternative ways of forming themselves to respond to the now and not have to react as if it is then.

I use the metaphor of a blueprint. A blueprint is a pattern that is used for replication. What if how you formed yourself in your response to sexual abuse made the blueprint? As a child, it helped you survive the experience as you would know what to do and when to do it. It was an important and essential tool. Go forward into adulthood. We can't take away the experience and I don't want to ignore the blueprint but I do want to review the blueprint and adapt it. If part of a client's response then in the blueprint was to hold their breath to manage their fear if anyone crossed their boundary, then that may be where they need to start because they know how to do that. The difference here is that holding their breath is the starting point and not the end point. When a client is aware that they are holding their breath, they may be able to recognize that they have a choice. They can stay holding their breath or they can consciously take a breath, and then if they feel the need to, they can hold their breath again. They have started to adapt the blueprint by responding and not just reacting. Using the same principle, it can help clients start to listen to their needs and begin to express them.

What I have described above may sound simplistic but survivors of childhood sexual abuse have managed far more in their survival than being asked to take a breath. I know it isn't that simple because along with taking a breath, the client has to notice themselves, their needs and their wants. A legacy of childhood sexual abuse is the sense of self being eradicated by the abuse, so, consciously, taking a breath is huge and as a therapist I see and feel that.

As a therapist to survivors of childhood sexual abuse, I will see what you want to show me and hear what you want to tell me.

I end here with a different metaphor, this time it's about therapy. When a client enters therapy they are holding the end of a rope and ask the therapist to hold the other end and be a trusted guide. As a therapist I will hold the end of the rope. I will be curious and ask the client to be curious too. When a client responds and consciously takes that breath, they can know that their therapist is holding the other end of the rope and they are survivors and can move beyond just surviving to thriving.

Willis

It was a conversation with a dear friend that echoed sentiments from my therapist, when I was 18 years old, and started my journey to become a counsellor. Childhood trauma shaped a significant amount of who I thought I was, well into my twenties.

I share the above because, for many of us survivors, the toxic voices from our pasts often bellow or ripple loudest in our day-to-day experiences and belief about who we are and who we will ever become.

Giving voice to the legacy of childhood sexual abuse by sharing my experiences from the position as a counsellor, group work facilitator and counsellor supervisor is done in a bid to offer insight from survivor and practitioner perspectives. Unfortunately, the breadth of what can be shared in this piece will only offer a glimpse of my path; however, I invite you to hear my words as encouragement to continue 'giving voice' to your story.

I will share elements of my counsellor, group work facilitator and counsellor supervisor support roles using three themes: individual work, group work, and supervision. In each element I will reflect on the significance of remaining client centred.

Individual work

Many years ago, as a newly qualified counsellor, I worked with a male survivor of sexual abuse of white European ethnicity. In fact, we were of the same generation and in our early twenties but from different sides of the socio-economic track; he came from a family where both parents were professionals. He had been given different mental health diagnoses that required prescribed medication, and at his most distressing points had experienced short periods of voluntary hospitalization. He had been revolving around the mental health system since his 14th birthday, but he had not told anyone about his history of sexual abuse. He was the only child, lived with his parents, and his mother was his abuser.

I recall our counselling sessions vividly and how I tried to show him how connected I was with his experience but never told him that I was a survivor too. This element of our counselling relationship was a point of contention for me for many weeks. I viewed myself as a person-centred counsellor who was genuine, empathic and accepting of everyone I worked with; however, there I was withholding this side of myself from our relationship.

The key questions for me were: in whose interest would I be sharing this part of myself and what benefit would this disclosure have for him in his therapy? A significant part of my reflecting on this dilemma in supervision related to him talking about how isolated he felt and the fact he had not told anyone else before sharing his history with me. I kept hearing the voice of my counsellor training lecturers saying 'be congruent...be real with the client'. They never told me that being real meant having such a deep understanding of my feelings that allowed me to be real in my expression, yet not unintentionally direct the client. Those few weeks felt like the longest, soul-searching period of my short counsellor career thus far. I found myself remembering my own abuse history during the counselling sessions, and constantly aiming to balance my silences, words, eye contact, gestures, and even how I dressed, so as not to block or lead the client. I did not want to mute the client's voice but I wanted him to know that I genuinely understood him more than he might even have thought.

Finally, through supervision, personal therapy and reading, I began to understand that so much of what occurs in counselling happens at a depth in the relationship where few words exist. Certainly, I found myself becoming more attuned through my eye contact and gestures. So, when I finally told the client that I too was a survivor, it was during a session where I looked into his eyes with a warm, fixed and unwavering level of contact and said, in a gentle yet firm tone, 'I genuinely... understand what you are saying. I...genuinely...understand.' My eyes became moist and I felt a wave of tenderness and care for him rise from my stomach; each word seemed to contain the depth of my self-disclosure. The session seemed to move in slow motion as we held direct contact through our gaze. He responded with 'Thank you'. In essence, I had stayed with him and done enough work on myself to offer him a real relationship that conveyed my vulnerability and awareness of maintaining boundaries, so he could attend to his own task of healing. I believe, as survivors, we learn to mistrust our emotions as a guiding force due to the betrayal of trust experienced during abuse. One of our tasks is to reconnect and give voice, once we understand our self in the context of each specific relationship. In this case, it was my self-understanding of this particular client gained through reflective supervision and a realization that counselling is dynamically relational, not formulaic like a mathematical equation.

The psychological depth of relational contact with clients is not exclusive to individual therapy. As a counsellor, I apply the art of professional reflection and reflexivity. I aim to remain aware of my potential actions or non-action in relation to clients. I must reflexively be aware of the social, cultural and economic contexts, to name a few, that the client exists within. Equally, awareness of the impact of each intervention must be considered when viewing the client as a whole person. In this regard, group work may be a useful testing ground for clients to explore their sense of self in a pseudo community, which is in the form of a therapy group. Although group members join groups based on a shared theme, for example survivors of sexual abuse, each brings their own unique story, experiences and biased views of the world to the community (group). Being aware of the shadows that sexual abuse may cast across a client's identity in relation to others, albeit others with a similar story, calls for creating spaces where all voices are welcome.

Group work

I have been fortunate enough to have developed and facilitated a range of group work sessions for male survivors of sexual abuse over the years. While men's group work is a dynamic process containing a diverse range of individual men's stories, hopes and expectations, themes of 'seeking kinship' are regularly expressed. The simple need of wanting to meet and share perspectives can be met through practical tasks – the life force of the group is the unpredictable dimension.

Each group member brings his own understanding of his experience to the group, with the usual interwoven threads of keeping secrets, conflicting feelings of responsibility and being tricked, self-doubt, isolation and so on. We then tightly sew sexual identity, gender roles and masculinities into the fabric of sexual abuse, and survivorship for male survivors creates complexity. Not that sexual abuse of males somehow conflicts with the impact of female sexual abuse survivors, rather that the complexity is in the way stereotypes of men as strong, powerful and unemotional may silence male survivors. Such stereotypes become a way of anchoring men to remain silent for decades. Giving voice to male survivors in groups enables men to reduce isolation and challenge the stereotypes that have bound them in silence. However, stereotypes also forge barriers between male survivors, with silence, isolation and lack of trust being key features.

Many male survivors whom I have worked with in groups have spoken of the dread and shame they experience in even signing up for a group. Their thoughts are of being shamed by other men, regardless of the thread of sexual abuse that binds them together, as stereotypes are sewn into their definitions of who they are. Men speak of remembering and, sometimes experiencing, flashbacks in the form of visual, hearing, taste, smell and physical sensations connected to the sexual abuse and/or taunting by peers, when joining groups. Such personal and unspoken obstacles become barriers to engaging in group work.

My approach to group work is to engage the adult male survivors with their younger selves. By this I mean their inner child, that part of the adult that is connected to childhood.

The introduction of creative-expressive interventions enables male survivors to begin to participate in group work from a place within themselves that is calling to be given a space to be heard, seen and acknowledged. Creative-expressive approaches include the use of music, poetry, drawing individually, in pairs and as part of a group, a community of male survivors.

As a facilitator, I enter the community and allow myself to be seen too. An example of such kinship is illustrated through the use of music in group work processes. During the life of the group, apart from the first and last sessions, each group member is invited to select a piece of music, from whatever genre he chooses. In the first session, either I or my co-facilitator model the process, by sharing a piece of music chosen for that specific group. For instance, I chose a track by Peter Gabriel called 'Don't Give Up', to symbolize the purpose of the group, and the lyrics conveyed my own struggle at times to remain confident or focused on my own healing. The group rule for this approach is that, if possible, the person who is sharing says why the track was chosen. The other group rules are that all group members remain silent while the track is playing; when it ends, no one is to offer interpretations or applause. Our aim is to accept what has been shared by simply saying 'thank you'. A note is taken by me or my co-facilitator of the artist, track name and which group member chose it. Each group member is then invited to share a music track each week and the pattern is repeated until the penultimate group session. In time for the last group session, all the tracks are compiled into a digital soundtrack and given a title using one word only. For instance, one group soundtrack was called 'Being', as that was a key word used during the life of the group. In the last group session, either me or my co-facilitator play the entire soundtrack while the group members create a community image on one large canvas or paper base, using chunky wax crayons, marker pens, chalks and oil pastels to write or draw their journey within the group. This is done while their soundtrack is playing so the images and tracks become anchored as a shared memory of their encounter of giving voice to their experiences as male survivors of sexual abuse.

Supervision

The use of creative-expressive approaches is significant when supporting female and male survivors of sexual abuse, as sometimes there are no words for what has been experienced. By this I mean, for some survivors, at the time of the abuse, they may have been so young that they didn't have any concept or spoken language to define their experience. Therefore, asking someone to tell me what they felt, when they do not have words, may become a shaming process.

Throughout the two examples above, reference has been given to supervision. The practice of supervision is key to offering the client and counsellor space to be psychologically held. There is also a core component of oversight to ensure that the counsellor (supervisee) remains focused on the client's needs with few interruptions to psychological contact. In my experience, regular themes in supervision revolve around the supervisee's drive towards offering the clients the best service possible. However, in doing so exists psychological aspects that are often referenced under the broad heading of 'transference', which can be both positive and negative. In the context of supervision, transference is actively used by the supervisor to develop an understanding of the supervisee's work. The dynamic part of the supervisory relationship emerges through the 'reactive' and 'proactive' counter-transference responses.

Such responses are based on the supervisor's professional and personal depth of reflection.

While supervising supervisees within sexual abuse survivor services, I must have an understanding of the training and personal aspects of the supervisee. These are important because every response I share with a supervisee will either encourage or discourage openness in our relationship, thus making the client visible or absent from the supervision process. There will be times when I feel an appropriate response is to share snippets of my professional or personal experiences with a supervisee while attending to the transference. My aim in such instances is to offer the supervisee a learning opportunity in our supervision session related to their client work that facilitates deeper reflection and reflexivity.

For instance, while supervising an experienced counsellor, I felt (counter-transference) that the supervisee was encountering a block in the therapy he was offering. He spoke of the client being 'stuck' and 'not wanting to progress'. My knowledge of the client and the male supervisee from previous supervisions informed my proactive response. The female client's story was one of having been sexually abused as an adult within a longstanding relationship, where repeated non-consensual sexual intercourse was a feature of the relationship. As the supervisee spoke, I heard the word 'no' repeatedly in my head. He had not said it, but the word was present in our supervision session. I asked whether the client had reported having said 'no' to her abuser. The supervisee paused for a few moments and replied, 'No, she hadn't.' My next enquiry was directed personally to the supervisee, as I asked him, 'How easy do you find it to say "no" to others?' The supervisee reported that he would usually avoid potentially confrontational situations and imply his objection when placed in a yes/no situation. This was the proactive aspect of supervision. I was able to raise awareness through a personal aspect of the supervisee's world and then worked with him to connect his personal self to his professional self.

As the client was not in the supervision session, yet she was central to the process, I worked with the supervisee to integrate his awareness beyond a spoken response. I invited him to place his hand on his chest and say 'no' and then to take his hand away and say 'no'. This was repeated several times, with him moving his hand slightly to different parts of his chest. I also invited him to say 'no' louder and louder so he could experience the force of his voice. The aim here was to facilitate the supervisee to feel what saying 'no' felt like for him, and equally to offer an opportunity to have his process witnessed and acknowledged. As he said 'no', he was visibly moved and became emotional. I reflected to him what I saw in the moment. His emotional response increased to the point of him becoming tearful, as he said, 'This is about me. I've been blocked.'

My role as supervisor is not to enter into therapy with supervisees; however, there are instances where the supervisory relationship becomes a facilitative process and personal therapy work is identified for supervisees. This was one such instance, as the personal knowledge the supervisee had shared in previous supervision identified his own survivorship of sexual abuse. In essence, the block he reported as the client's process was in fact an aspect of his personal experience that had been re-awakened (counter-transference) through his work with this particular client.

Reintegration of knowledge gained through supervision of the supervisee's client work was discussed. We reflected on how the supervisee may introduce his increased self-knowledge and the facilitative intervention we had shared together in his client work. This was a significant facet of the supervision process, as it was about ownership of his work, and not simply imitation, since the therapeutic relationship is forged on realness.

Individual, group and supervisory dimensions of therapy with survivors of sexual abuse require a depth of self-awareness and courage to face our own shadows. After all, we are inviting clients to shed light on dark corners of their psyche. We are not observers or processors of psychological pain. I believe that in every encounter with a client or supervisee, within individual or group settings, we are charged with a duty to engage with courage. Such courage is beyond the reading of articles or watching video clips. The dynamic relational contact, through reflection being witnessed and acknowledged, affords us spaces in which our psychological and emotional worlds may be enriched by giving voice from within.

CHAPTER 2

Themes

The narratives demonstrate the range of child sexual abuse within the family as well as the child's psychosocial world. Many survivors were sexually abused by a parent or parental figure, including fathers and grandfathers, as well as mothers (*Maud*), and in the case of Candice, an older sibling. Some of the survivors were abused by people outside the family (*Matt, Lucy, Alastair*). While there are some commonalities in the narratives, they are also testament that survivors' experiences are not homogenous and there is a need to view each survivor through the lens of their own unique lived experience by listening to and hearing survivors' own words, and viewing them as experts in their lived experience.

One survivor (*Candice*) experienced sibling sexual abuse and highlights the difficulty of disclosure of this and the responses to it. Sibling sexual abuse has historically been under-reported and under-researched. This is in part due to the lack of understanding of what constitutes typical sexual development and atypical sexual development in which sexual behaviour between siblings is seen as a natural part of sexual experimentation (Sanderson, 2004). As Candice's narrative demonstrates, many survivors of SSA report that when they have disclosed their abuse to parents or professionals, this has been minimized and ascribed to normal sexual development and thus not abusive.

Despite SSA being considered to be the most common form of child sexual abuse within the family setting in the UK, it remains a hidden, chronically underestimated and untreated form of child sexual abuse. It continues to be ignored, played down or denied by parents, professionals and authorities as harmless or non-threatening childhood sexual experimentation that is less serious or impactful than generational sexual abuse (McCartan, Anning & Qureshi, 2021). It is claimed that because the harmful sibling is a child, they are not aware of what they are doing, and as such are not fully responsible for their sexual behaviour. Clearly there needs to be more research into SSA and CSA committed by children to fully understand the dynamics inherent in this form of abuse and ensure that both the victim and the perpetrator are appropriately supported.

It is clear that CSA leaves long-lasting wounds which continue to exert considerable influence into adulthood. The predominant impact of CSA on survivors consists of trauma reactions which elicit a range of emotional, cognitive and interpersonal responses such as fear, anxiety, shame, loss of identity, confusion and isolation. These commonly manifest in emotional dysregulation, hyper- and hypoarousal, compromised mental and physical health, loss of sense of self, impaired relationships and sexuality, lack of educational attainment and vocational stability, as well as reduced life choices such as fear of having children. These responses may be exacerbated if there is identity-based trauma as a result of CSA, such as masculinity in male survivors or if the survivor has also experienced racism, marginalization or other form of stigmatization. Practitioners need to be mindful of how these intersect with CSA and the concomitant impact on the survivor.

One of the main themes that survivors of CSA expressed in these narratives was about not having a voice and feeling silenced. Another common theme was needing to protect family members, including the abuser, and fear of the devastation that would result through disclosure. Disclosure was fraught with difficulties, with many survivors not being believed, or being asked to retract their claims, or being scapegoated. In many cases, this led to loss of the family, and, for some, having to leave the country in which they were raised. Given these complex family dynamics, many survivors report having to live a double life in order to navigate family interactions and manage the impact of CSA.

Many survivors report how hard it is to access specialist therapeutic services and how they were often misunderstood and misdiagnosed by professionals who were not able to link behaviour and presenting symptoms to a history of CSA. Some survivors felt that this lack of understanding from some mental health professionals and generic, short-term counselling left them feeling more vulnerable, making it harder to seek further help. Conversely, those survivors who felt heard and understood by professionals found that they were able to gradually heal and recover from their abuse.

The most common themes in this research provide an opportunity for developing a deeper understanding of the lived experience of survivors of CSA. In addition, some of these themes reflect and concur with some of the recurring themes that have been highlighted in the research and clinical literature.

Narrative themes
Silence and secrecy
The need for secrecy and silence to protect family members, including the abuser, means leading a double life in which

external reality differs markedly from internal reality (*Muriel, Lou, Maud, Chris, Matt, Samia, Alastair, Reena*). Alongside this, the betrayal of trust, lack of boundaries, unpredictability and uncertainty lead to confusion and a range of emotional and cognitive responses, including shame. Over time, distorted perceptions and behaviour become normalized (*Anthea, Maud, Chris, Lucy, Candice*).

As CSA is shrouded in secrecy, it makes it extremely hard to break the silence, talk about the abuse or disclose for fear of consequences. The ongoing process of CSA is punctuated by a series of daily challenges, such as maintaining the secret and overwhelming feelings with no source of comfort. It means having to become invisible to avoid the abuse and hide the shame, and developing a false self to hide the wounded inner self. In addition, the child has to make sense of how to behave at night and what is expected during the day. This creates the merciless paradox of knowing and not knowing: knowing that something is wrong and the need *not to know* for fear of what that might unleash.

In addition, the child fears being close to others in case the secret is exposed. This leads to a fear of making friends or developing close relationships, which can persist into adulthood and lead to isolation and loneliness as they fear reaching out or connecting with others and instead become locked in a psychological prison. Not being able to engage in or sustain friendships means that the child will not develop the requisite relational skills in childhood to support relationships in adulthood.

Many of the survivors (*Anthea, Maud, Chris, Lucy, Candice*) reported the need to remain silent and keep the secret. To ensure that the abuse remained hidden, many survivors had to deny it to themselves and others, often to protect siblings, the non-abusing parent(s) and the abuser, for fear of the consequences of exposure. Keeping the secret of the abuse necessitates denial in order to suppress the pain and shame, as well as keeping reality at bay (Sanderson, 2019a).

As mentioned above, many survivors felt that to keep the secret they had to lead a complex double life in which their external reality was in stark contrast to their internal reality. This would commonly involve wearing a happy, smiling mask to cover the hurt and pain inside. Many of the survivors felt betrayed by their abuser, and some felt let down by other family members who were unable to read the signs of abuse, or failed to believe them or to act when a disclosure was made. This led to a deep sense of abandonment in which they felt like psychological orphans.

The ripple effect can reverberate throughout the whole family, as everyone is drawn into a *folie en famille* in order to keep the secret and prevent the truth from being exposed. Alongside this, some survivors were prevented from having a relationship with the non-abusing parent in order to minimize the risk of exposing the abuse, while others withdrew from close relationships with others to ensure that the secret would not be revealed inadvertently.

Speaking the unspeakable: communication and giving voice

Speaking the unspeakable is hard, especially for young children who do not have the language or cognitive capacity. This is particularly the case if the child is pre-verbal when the abuse occurs, and because traumatic experiences are stored in the right brain and are harder to access verbally. As a result, many survivors are not able to communicate or give voice to their experiences and end up sending non-verbal or somatic signals, or speak in coded messages. It is essential that practitioners are aware of this and find ways of decoding messages without shaming the survivors, or find alternative ways to encourage them to give voice to their experiences and communicate through expressive and creative therapies.

The need for silence and not being able to give voice to or to talk about their experiences prevents reality checking and processing. It also impairs communication of what is being experienced, which can persist into adulthood. As children, they know there is something wrong but they are not allowed to know as this would endanger them further. As their needs are ignored, or not permitted a voice, any attempts to communicate are usually heavily coded or tied up in riddles. This can often manifest in the therapeutic session where the survivor is not able to say what they wish to say other than in code in the hope that the therapist can decode it. Alternatively, many survivors hope that others, including the therapist, will be able to 'mind read' what happened and what is being experienced internally rather than the survivor having to say it. This can be challenging for the therapist, especially when focusing on clarity of expression. Practitioners need to understand that coded messages and the desire for someone to mind read are protective strategies in childhood and when used in adulthood are a sign of fear and shame. Practitioners must manage this sensitively in a paced, collaborative way to gain meaning rather than judge the survivor, so that they can gain confidence in their voice.

Disclosure

Keeping the secret makes disclosure extremely difficult, especially if the abuser is someone within or known to the family.

Fear of not being believed, and the consequences of breaking the silence, exerts immense pressure on the child (and later adult) to protect the family, including the abuser. Many survivors weigh up the need to reveal the secret with the impact this might have on the family and the fear of hurting others. If the abuser is a much-loved family member such as a parent, older sibling or grandparent, they do not want to hurt the abuser or see him or her go to prison.

Many of the survivors wrote about the difficulties surrounding disclosure, with several reporting that multiple attempts at disclosure were made, and that initial disclosures made in childhood were often misunderstood, disbelieved or ignored, not just by the family but also by professionals (*Muriel, Lou, Anthea, Maud, Lucy, Samia, Candice, Alastair*). For some, later disclosures were heard but often accompanied by being blamed for destroying or bringing shame on the family. Some survivors worked very hard to protect the family and the abuser to keep the family together, and only broke the silence when they could no longer hold the secret, or after the abuser died.

Some survivors feared being re-traumatized through breaking the silence. Many survivors who broke the silence felt that the abuse was either dismissed, trivialized or minimized, and they were blamed for breaking up the family. Those survivors who were disowned by their families often felt shame and blamed themselves for their family's disintegration.

A few survivors found support from siblings and the non-abusing parent when breaking the silence as adults, and some were able to reconcile and rebuild the relationship with the non-abusing parent. Thus, disclosure and breaking the silence is fraught with danger and can have long-lasting consequences such as re-traumatization and the irrevocable loss of the family.

Disclosure is invariably fraught with fear and anxiety and multiple attempts are often made to break the silence, especially when the secret becomes too big to handle. In our narratives, first disclosures were often met with disbelief, or ignored, while later disclosures, some not until after the abuser's death, were also judged, leaving the survivor with a further sense of betrayal. The impact of disclosure invariably had a significant impact on all family members, with some families severing all contact with the survivor, although some were able to gain positive support from siblings and the non-abusing parent.

A corollary to this is disclosure and reporting to the police. A number of the survivors (*Lou, Anthea, Chris, Lucy*) did report the CSA to the police only to find that it was unsuccessful or failed to progress, while others felt negatively impacted as the investigations were often extremely protracted.

Leading a double life

The dynamics of CSA are predicated on deception and the distortion of reality which leads to confusion around love and abusive behaviour. As responsibility for the abuse is often projected onto the survivor, implying that they wanted it, or they are made to feel complicit in the abuse, the child's reality is distorted. The paradox of knowing that something is wrong yet being told that it is normal, or having to deny that it is abuse, leads to many survivors having to fabricate a complex double life, in which they either became invisible or construct a mask or façade to cover up reality (*Muriel, Anthea, Chris, Matt, Samia, Reena*). These masks commonly consist of pretending to be someone else, or appearing to be normal and happy by smiling, complying and people-pleasing to cover up the internal sense of chaos, confusion and worthlessness (Sanderson, 2015a, 2019a).

This persona enables the survivor to connect with others, albeit on a surface level, as being too close would expose the real self lurking beneath the mask. The pretence, enabling them to become a chameleon, often extends into adulthood wherein they continue to hide their real self.

Distortion of reality and confusion

A common theme in the narratives was confusion and the distortion of reality, which is often reinforced by abusers who blame the survivor for the abuse, or imply that CSA is a normal part of a special and loving relationship. In this distortion, the world is turned upside down, nothing makes sense and there is nothing to hold on to. To manage the distortion, survivors have to adapt their behaviour and sense of self to fit what has been imposed on them. As a result, they become compliant and develop a negative self-identity, or a 'false self' in which they blame themselves for their abuse.

In addition, confusion and 'not knowing' lead to 'mind reading' the abuser so the child can brace and prepare themselves for the next assault. The need to know bestows a semblance of control and acts as a protective survival strategy. In keeping the secret, the survivor will need to lie, which further undermines their sense of self.

Abusers are more powerful if they can induce confusion and chaos as this makes the child more dependent on them. Commonly, abusers distort the child's reality by making them feel special and proclaiming that the abuse is a way of showing how much they love the child. In being made to feel special, the child can feel a sense of power, when in reality they are powerless. In addition, the pretence of caring masks the annihilation of the child's self. Abusers also make the child feel complicit in their abuse by suggesting that they 'wanted it' or 'liked it'. Furthermore, the implication is that the child has a choice, when in reality there is no choice at all. In being made to feel responsible for the CSA, the survivor blames themselves, leading to a deeply felt sense of shame and self-loathing. The fear of exposure of how 'bad' they are in causing the abuse reinforces the need to lead a double life in which they are seen as a 'good child' (*Anthea*).

While the distortion of reality and the deformation of self allows some survivors to hide their true feelings in order to remain connected to the family, it invariably exerts a huge cost through the loss of self-identity and authenticity. The legacy of this is manifested in distorted perceptions of self and others and a permanent sense of confusion in which nothing makes sense, and their hold on reality became even more tenuous, increasing self-doubt and lack of trust in themselves.

Denial

Denial is an effective strategy at the time of the CSA as it enables the child to keep the secret of what happened to them. It also allows the survivor to deny or minimize the harm done and impact of the CSA (*Lou, Candice, Alastair*) by blocking out memories, dissociating and suppressing feelings such as sadness, anger or rage. This denial is further reinforced by others, especially the abuser or family members, or professionals who prefer to dismiss the CSA by labelling the survivor as attention seeking, mentally unwell or unstable, or a fantasist.

Lack of trust

The repeated betrayal in CSA leads to a basic lack of trust in self and others, which was expressed by many survivors (*Muriel, Lou, Anthea, Maud, Chris, Samia, Candice, Alastair*), with Samia relaying that as a result of the abuse she never felt safe. This is often accompanied by the need to be liked, accepted and understood, which can lead survivors to trust too easily, even when there is no evidence of trustworthiness, and can increase the risk of being abused or victimized again.

Many of the survivors described how hard it was to trust themselves or others, and how this led to self-doubt (*Muriel, Anthea, Maud, Chris, Samia, Candice*). While many do find it hard to trust, some trust too quickly in the hope that this will be honoured and that they will not be harmed. Survivors who find it hard to trust will commonly test others to see whether they can be trusted, including their therapist. Trust is best viewed on a spectrum rather than a binary polarized 'trust' and 'no trust', and is a process that evolves over time with varying degrees of trust that can alter depending on the course of the relationship.

Due to impaired trust, many survivors expressed being terrified of people and not being able to trust others, which often led to avoidance and withdrawal from others, leading to self-imposed isolation and unbearable loneliness. Shame and fear meant that they had difficulties socializing, or engaging in or sustaining relationships, as their need for predictability, certainty, control and their lack of spontaneity made it difficult to be responsive to care and affection.

While many survivors yearn to trust, be loved and cared for, they are often terrified, or suspicious of this, as love and care means being abused and hurt. Many survivors struggle to accept being loved, despite desperately seeking this, and as they cannot accept let alone like themselves, they find it hard to believe that others might like or care for them.

A number of survivors can only relate through compulsively putting other people's needs first, or helping others, as this enables them to feel more in control. As many feel they are unable to trust others, express their needs or set boundaries, they often find relationships difficult and exhausting, with some avoiding relationships and intimacy. A good example of this is Maud, who has never formed any friendships, let alone an intimate relationship. The inability to trust others and terror of intimacy means that some survivors become fiercely self-reliant and self-sufficient as they mask their vulnerability with a sense of invincibility and a disavowal of their need for others. Such survivors often reject or devalue any help that is offered by shifting their sense of shame away from themselves on to others (Sanderson, 2019a).

Sense of self and self-identity

An experience common to all survivors was the loss of self and loss of self-identity which was felt to be soul destroying (*Muriel, Anthea, Maud, Chris, Matt, Lucy, Alastair*). Many survivors felt as if a part of the self was missing, lost or broken and that their identity had been damaged and corrupted. They felt different from everyone else and experienced a sense of worthlessness, powerlessness, self-loathing and self-hatred (*Lou, Matt*). They also reported feeling 'unlovable' (*Muriel, Maud*), dirty, bad, defective and worthless (*Anthea, Maud, Matt*) and lacking in self-esteem (*Chris, Lucy*) and self-confidence (*Alastair*).

The lack of self prompted many to wear a mask to cover up their inner pain, or render themselves invisible. This is a way to blend in so they can remain under the radar and not draw attention to themselves. This chameleon-like protective strategy enabled them to adapt to whatever others expected of them (*Alastair*), leading to a precarious and discordant sense of self. Being in a constant state of flux creates uncertainty and doubt which prevents the development of a cohesive sense of self. The capriciousness and fluctuation of the self hinders the survivor from trusting themselves, rendering them more vulnerable to be moulded by others.

Many survivors are scared to be themselves for fear of being seen as vulnerable, worthless, flawed or powerless. These survivors describe themselves as being trapped in two emotional worlds, one of anger and the other of shame, which they have to conceal. They are afraid to be themselves, or show their true feelings or needs (*Reena*), for fear of hurting others, being seen as bad or selfish, or being subjected to further rejection (*Alastair*). This means adopting a mask of invulnerability and being in control as a way to hide their thoughts, feelings and needs. Many survivors are too scared and ashamed to be themselves, or to live (*Maud*), and as a result feel that their lives are not fully lived and that they have to lead a double life to protect themselves (Sanderson, 2015a, 2016).

In the absence of a core self-identity, some survivors become vulnerable to adopting a victim or survivor identity, which can be self-limiting. This can hold them hostage to defining themselves solely as survivors of CSA rather than it being something that happened to them which does not define who they are or the whole of the self.

Negative self-perception, self-thoughts and self-talk

The self-blame and shame felt by many survivors impact on their perception of self and their self-identity. This is seen in feelings of self-loathing and self-hatred, a lack of dignity or honour, feeling like 'damaged goods' or feeling that they are so flawed that others will be repulsed by them (*Muriel, Lou, Anthea, Maud, Matt, Lucy, Candice, Alastair*). This negative view of the self is often supported by negative self-talk (*Muriel, Anthea, Matt, Lucy*). This negative self-perception can lead to automatic negative thoughts, self-criticism and ruminations (*Muriel, Lou, Anthea, Maud, Matt, Lucy, Candice, Alastair*), which can be so corrosive that some survivors feel they have no right to exist. This increases dependency on others to value them and shore up their self-esteem, which further reinforces a sense of shame and powerlessness.

Negative thoughts and beliefs are often inflamed by trauma and heightened anxiety, and are more likely to consist of biased thinking as the person is in survival mode and not able to fully engage in objective cognitive processing. As a result, survivors of CSA are more vulnerable to misjudgements that tend to reinforce fears or anxieties and prolong pain and misery. Negative beliefs and distorted thinking are sometimes so habitual that they become automatic and seem to occur outside awareness. Some negative beliefs are distorted perceptions inserted by the abuser(s) which could not be challenged as a child and are therefore incorporated into the survivor's belief system.

Negative self-beliefs such as 'I am to blame', 'I am bad', 'I am worthless', 'I am unlovable', 'I am a failure' or 'I am dirty and filthy' infect the developing self-identity and can lead to the survivor seeing the world through the abuser's eyes, voice and actions. As these become incorporated into their core sense of self, survivors may not even be aware of their negative thoughts or their impact.

Negative self-beliefs are reflected in the inner critical voice, which constantly undermines the survivor and acts as a saboteur who prevents the development of any self-esteem. They can also lead to the false belief that as they were to blame for the abuse, they deserve all the bad things that happen to them.

Some survivors engage in endless rumination, or covert compulsions, in which negative and shameful thoughts about harming others or having committed appalling crimes are repeatedly replayed in their head. These ruminations tend to be self-censoring and corrosive, and extremely exhausting and time consuming, making it hard for a survivor to engage in other activities, go to work or live life fully.

To compensate for perceived flaws, many survivors impose unrealistic expectations on themselves, leading to a need to be perfect to compensate for their perceived deficiencies and concomitant shame. As the expectations in perfectionist thinking and behaviour are unrealistic and virtually impossible to achieve, the survivor is inevitably destined to fail. This reinforces the sense of failure, guilt and self-criticism – and the cycle continues.

Dissociation

A common trauma reaction is dissociation (*Muriel, Lou, Anthea, Maud, Chris, Matt, Samia, Candice, Alastair*), an adaptive psychobiological survival strategy that anaesthetizes the traumatic impact of CSA by numbing painful experiences and feelings. Dissociation, while adaptive at the time of the abuse, ultimately leads to confusion (*Maud, Samia, Candice*), lack of focus, fragmented memories and an increased sense of unreality. For some survivors, dissociation becomes a permanent state as 'natural as breathing' as it suppresses feelings such as despair, anger and rage. This can lead to an avoidance of all feelings, including pleasure and joy, as it is not possible to numb selectively. While dissociation numbs the emotional pain by suppressing feelings, memories and the reality of the abuse, it can lead to fragmented memories, making it harder to validate the abuse.

This sense of numbness was variously described by our survivors as feeling 'unreal', being 'zoned out' or 'living in a fog' (*Muriel, Anthea, Maud, Chris, Matt, Samia, Candice*). These are classic signs of dissociation. Several survivors reported that 'zoning out' impaired their concentration, which prevented them from reaching their full potential with regard to academic attainment and later vocational opportunities, as well as the processing of memories of the abuse.

Many survivors describe 'disconnecting from' or 'leaving' their body during the abuse and watching themselves from above, as though it was happening to someone else. In trying to blunt the impact of trauma and ongoing threat, they become hypoaroused in order not to feel or experience anything. Dissociation is characterized by two core symptoms: depersonalization and derealization. In depersonalization the survivor's sense of self and identity becomes confused, resulting in a loss of the sense of who they are, or feeling estranged from their body and feeling it is unreal, changing or dissolving. They can also become detached from their body and have out-of-body experiences, or feel as though they are watching themselves in a dream or film rather than actually experiencing what is happening to them. This deletion from the body can feel frightening, which compounds the need to dissociate.

Alongside this, survivors may feel estranged from their surroundings through derealization, in which the world seems unreal, the familiar is unfamiliar, friends become unreal or turn into robots, and objects appear to change in shape, size or colour. The overall experience is saturated with vague and dreamlike states which are typically described by survivors as being in a haze or living in a fog (*Maud*).

With repeated trauma, dissociation can become a way of life, and what started as an adaptive way of coping with trauma becomes harmful as the survivor loses touch with their thoughts, emotions, sensations and memories. This prevents them from making sense of their experiences and being able to develop a coherent narrative of the abuse. Over time, this can become a default setting wherein the survivor is so disconnected from sensations and feelings that they no longer inhabit their body and can only live in their head. This fear of feeling (*Chris, Matt, Candice*) means that all feelings need to be suppressed, including positive feelings as these are often associated with the negative experiences of CSA, and so must be eradicated. This leads some survivors to turn to substances such as food, alcohol or drugs to keep them in a state of numbness and hypoarousal (Sanderson, 2019a).

Persistent and chronic dissociation can lead to aspects of the self or personality becoming fragmented and splintered into separate identities or parts. In structural dissociation, the self splits into what feels like two personalities: the Apparently Normal Personality (ANP), which is extremely high functioning, and the Emotional Personality (EP), which is often overwhelmed by emotions and much less able to function (Sanderson, 2013a; van der Hart, Nijenhuis & Steele, 2006). When in the ANP state, the survivor has disavowed all aspects of the trauma and split off all associated feelings. In contrast, when in the EP state, the survivor is overwhelmed with floods of trauma-associated feelings. In separating the two they are able to be more functional to manage their daily lives when in the ANP mode. When in the EP mode they are overwhelmed and less able to function.

This split is commonly associated with high-functioning clients who are out of contact with their unresolved trauma. Although they often present as emotionally literate, this is commonly a cover up for an internal emotional vacuum or emptiness. When they do talk about emotions these are rarely 'felt' and commonly represent 'thought' emotions in which the right emotion is cognitively identified rather than experienced. Over time, high-functioning survivors can develop what van der Hart *et al.* (2006) call 'a phobia of inner experience', which prevents them from integrating the trauma or linking their behaviour to their abuse experiences. Some survivors feel that being able to 'split themselves in two', with one part being functional and seeking to protect others while the other part was disintegrating, allowed them to survive the trauma (Sanderson, 2015b, 2019a). Some survivors experience multiple splits in their sense of self which can coalesce into separate personalities as seen in dissociative identity disorder.

Dissociation can account for a range of symptoms such as mood swings, personality shifts, forgetfulness, dreamlike states, and inattention or memory loss for periods of time, which can be frightening and distressing for a survivor if they can't remember where they were or what they were doing for some hours.

Shame

Shame is like a virus that infects the soul and is ubiquitous in survivors of CSA (*Lou, Anthea, Maud, Chris, Matt, Lucy, Samia, Candice, Alastair, Reena*), alongside guilt and self-blame. In shame, the very core of the person is affected, leading them to have to apologize for their existence. Shame is also the gatekeeper of secrets and powerful suppressed feelings that need to be hidden for fear that the shame is exposed.

CSA invariably engenders self-blame and shame, with survivors feeling dirty, worthless and inadequate. The narratives in this book demonstrate the corrosive nature of shame, which leaves an indelible stain on their sense of self-worth and self-esteem. The overwhelming feelings of self-loathing and self-disgust can only be quelled by pushing them out of conscious awareness, or disavowing the shame.

Shame is present not only at the time of the abuse, but also when the abuse is revealed and they fear being shamed by others. Shame during the abuse is commonly due to the nature of the sexual acts, having to submit to them and not being able to defend themselves. This is intensified if the child becomes sexually aroused or is forced to take on the abuser's shame and blame themselves.

Survivors may also feel shame for approaching the abuser(s), or going back to the abuser(s). It is crucial that survivors do not view this as evidence for wanting to have sexual contact but as a basic human need for connection. In addition, children sometimes approach the abuser(s) in order to have some control and predictability over the abuse. Approaching the abuser(s) is a survival strategy that makes the abuse more predictable and enables the child to arm themselves in preparation for the assault, as a way to protect themselves and feel less vulnerable. Similarly, if the survivor was aroused, or had an erection or orgasm during the CSA, this does not mean they wanted to be sexually abused or are responsible for it.

In self-blame, the child takes on the responsibility for the abuse in order to retain a positive image of the abuser on whom they depend for their survival. This self-blame is often heightened by the abuser telling the child it is their fault and that they made the abuser behave in a sexual way. As the abuser does not take any responsibility for the abuse, the child has no choice but to blame themselves.

Self-blame can have psychological benefits, such as allowing the child to believe that the abuser loves and cares for them. The child can form an image of the abuser as essentially good, whereas the child is bad. While this preserves a much-needed sense of attachment, it makes it harder to legitimize the abuse. Self-blame also allows for a sense of control in which the child can believe that 'if only I hadn't done this...then that wouldn't have happened', which induces a semblance of control in the face of potential abuse in the future and reduces their sense of helplessness and powerlessness.

Shame is also a powerful way for the abuser to control the child and reduce the risk of exposure. It is in the interest of the abuser to make the child feel guilty and ashamed as this ensures silence and secrecy, making it impossible for the child to tell anyone. In addition, in blaming themselves, the child is prevented from being in touch with the harm done and is more able to suppress any anger. As a consequence, the child takes on the blame, shame and the responsibility of the abuser.

Self-blame and shame invariably lead to self-loathing and negative evaluations commonly seen in critical thoughts and feelings about the self. Many survivors become shame-prone and highly sensitized to shame by persistently seeking confirmation of their shameworthiness or through negative self-evaluations and interminable shame-based ruminations.

Although shame can be healthy in regulating behaviour, chronic and pervasive shame is crippling as it can lead to a loss of self, and a sense of inadequacy and failure. It also prevents the development of a sense of healthy pride, spontaneity, pleasure and self-agency. Shame proneness is based on the entrenched belief that the self is bad or inadequate, which leads to a heightened sensitivity to shaming experiences, real or imagined. This is typically seen in hypervigilance to cues of shame in the use of language, and non-verbal communication such as body language, that confirm their shameworthiness.

This can be compounded when survivors experience vicarious shame, which is taking on the shame that the abuser has disavowed, or secondary shame, which is shame for their feelings (such as sadness or anxiety) and their emotional reactions (such as dependency needs or vulnerability), or shame for simply feeling ashamed.

A recurring conflict in shame is the need to be visible and the need to be invisible. To defend against shame, survivors may withdraw by hiding or isolating themselves, physically or psychologically. Alternatively, they may attack the self through negative talk and beliefs about the self, or self-shaming behaviours through activities that induce shame. Some survivors use self-deprecating humour to manage their shame, as exposing their shame in this way enables them to stay connected to others. Some avoid the feeling of shame by numbing it through the use of drugs or alcohol, or by covering it up with perfectionism, excessive pride, arrogance, grandiosity or narcissism. Narcissism and arrogance become effective ways of keeping people at bay, which reduces the risk of the shame being exposed. A further defence against shame is to attack others, whereby the focus of shame is deflected away from the survivor and projected onto others (Nathanson, 1992; Sanderson, 2015b).

Relationship difficulties

CSA, especially by a family member or someone who is supposed to love, nurture and protect the child, leads to fear of attachment and intimacy as relationships are experienced as sources of danger rather than safety. These narratives demonstrate how relationships are often fraught with difficulties such as lack of trust, the inability to say no or set boundaries or to express feelings and needs (*Muriel, Lou, Anthea, Maud, Matt, Lucy, Samia, Candice, Alastair*).

CSA hijacks the attachment system, making it extremely hard to trust others or get close to others, and the fear that closeness will be sexualized can lead to the avoidance of relationships (*Lou, Maud, Matt*). This creates a paradox in which the survivor yearns for closeness and yet is compelled to avoid it. As a result, survivors make themselves invisible in relationships to avoid getting hurt or being shamed, even though remaining invisible induces existential angst. This double bind of desire for intimacy and fear of being entrapped can cause difficulties in relationships and intimacy. This can lead survivors to either avoid intimacy, or propel them to be too trusting or over-intimate too quickly, making them more vulnerable to further betrayal or abuse.

The betrayal of trust and violation boundaries in CSA means that many survivors experience relationships as dangerous rather than a haven of safety or solace. As love is equated with harm and abuse, many survivors of CSA find it hard to trust others as they fear further abuse, betrayal or abandonment. As a result they get caught in a never-ending cycle of attempting to be close to others followed by pushing them away, which is both confusing and exhausting.

The lack of trust and fear of intimacy means that many survivors have difficulties in engaging and sustaining relationships

(*Muriel, Lou, Anthea, Maud, Matt, Lucy, Samia, Candice, Alastair*), as their need for predictability, certainty, control and lack of spontaneity makes it difficult to be responsive to care and affection. In addition, shame and negative self-perception make survivors suspicious of anyone who claims to love or care for them. To protect themselves they may be compelled to keep people at bay, often through anger or hostility. This anger is typically due to fear rather than aggression and requires empathy and compassion rather than judgement or punishment.

Some survivors may fear closeness and intimacy so intensely that they are unable to form any significant intimate relationships and remain isolated throughout their lives, which becomes a source of shame and 'proof' of their worthlessness (*Maud, Matt, Candice, Alastair*). The inability to trust others and terror of intimacy means that some survivors fear having children, which is experienced as a huge loss in later life (*Maud, Matt, Samia*).

The conditioned compliance and submissiveness in CSA typically translates into people-pleasing, in both childhood and adulthood. As a result, many survivors tolerate disrespectful behaviours as they are not sure how to set boundaries, either because they expect no better or they believe they deserve to be treated badly (*Samia, Candice, Alastair*). Not being able to say no to abusive behaviour makes them more vulnerable to re-victimization or being ensnared in exploitative relationships (Sanderson, 2013a, 2015b, 2019a, 2019b).

Many survivors believe that the only way to avoid being hurt or rejected is to please, rescue or fix others. This renders them more vulnerable to abusive relationships which are characterized by domination, or violence and coercive control. This leads to so-called 'co-dependency' in which the individual 'needs to be needed' and is often enmeshed with people who 'need to dominate' (Sanderson, 2019a). Survivors who fear dependency and who are vehemently self-reliant tend to mask their needs and vulnerability by controlling the behaviour of others or by repeating abusive patterns from childhood.

The masquerade of abuse as love and affection seen in CSA makes it difficult to know genuine love and nurturing. Survivors who did not experience love, warmth or nurturing as a child will believe that they are unlovable and will not know how to respond when this is offered, and will perceive tenderness and kindness as a prelude to pain. The message in CSA is that your only worth in relationships is to satisfy the needs or desires of others, primarily through sex. The fear of being in a relationship can extend to other relationships, such as family, friends, children, work colleagues and professional connections.

Sexuality

CSA commonly contaminates survivors' sexuality and ability to be sexual (*Muriel, Matt, Samia, Candice*) and gives rise to a range of sexual difficulties which can be distressing and affect sexual relationships. While some survivors experience little or no difficulties, others feel that their sexual lives have been forever damaged. The spectrum of sexual difficulties can range from suppressed sexuality and avoidance of sex through to indiscriminate sexual encounters. Some survivors become either hyposexual or hypersexual resulting in sexual acting out, promiscuity and compulsive sexual behaviour. In some cases, survivors experience confusion about their sexual orientation and preferences. Male survivors who have experienced CSA by males may have fears about their masculinity and compensate for this by adopting hyper-masculine behaviours.

These difficulties often represent aspects of the abuse in which avoiding sex is a way of saying no, which they were not able to in childhood, while compulsive sexual behaviour is often a re-enactment of the CSA experience, and as such is not experienced as pleasurable. Some survivors are only able to have sex under the influence of alcohol or drugs, while others become addicted to sex, or are lured into sex work by the abuser(s) or to fund their addiction (Sanderson, 2019b).

Survivors of CSA will invariably feel betrayed by their body. The lack of control over the body means that they feel hijacked by their body and feel they have no ownership over it (*Candice*). This is compounded by dissociation in which they have erased or deleted their body as a way of avoiding feelings and somatic sensations.

Survivors of CSA can feel betrayed by their body due to involuntary arousal during the sexual abuse, or because they felt pleasure, had an erection, became lubricated or had an orgasm. These are natural responses in the presence of sexual touch and do not necessarily indicate sexual desire. Erections can be involuntary and happen in a variety of situations, including fear and stress. Similarly, vaginal lubrication in females is an automatic biological reaction to minimize tissue damage. Survivors need to be able to distinguish between sexual arousal and sexual desire and recognize that one can be sexually aroused without the desire to be sexual, or to engage in sex. They also need to be aware that abusers often perform specific sexual acts to deliberately induce arousal and pleasure, leading the child to believe they wanted the sexual contact and thus blame themselves. This strategy makes it easier for the abuser(s) to shift responsibility for the abuse onto the child and therefore reduce the risk of disclosure.

For some survivors, such early sexualization can lead to a

greater sensitivity to sexual excitation and hypersexual arousal. This can lead to the child and later survivor to seek release of elevated levels of sexual energy through indiscriminate sexual encounters, and putting themselves more at risk of further abuse (*Candice*). This is compounded through the objectification of their body and the sense that their body does not belong to them and is the property of others. In addition, the pleasure of physical contact through affectionate hugs has become confused and tainted with the demands of being sexual, and satisfying someone else's needs.

The betrayal of the body can lead to body shame in which survivors want to hide their body by upholstering it through excess weight, or disfigurement, or they neglect personal hygiene to ward off sexual advances. Alternatively, some survivors may compensate for their feelings of shame by dressing and behaving in a sexually provocative way. Some survivors diet to excess or starve themselves to remain pre-pubertal (Sanderson, 2016), while male survivors may excessively body-build to compensate for feeling vulnerable and to protect against any future abuse. Some survivors may exercise excessively in order to gain control over a body they feel betrayed them during the CSA.

Many survivors struggle during sex as they become overwhelmed by powerful feelings of terror, shame, humiliation or anger, which they fear they cannot contain. They may experience flashbacks or intrusive memories during sexual stimulation which can lead to 'tuning out', or dissociation. This is because sexual intimacy triggers the same bodily sensations present during the abuse and activates the same feelings of terror and fear. This can elicit a range of protective reactions such as detachment, withdrawal and aggression, which can be frightening to both the survivor and their partner.

Addiction

There is a powerful interplay between trauma, dissociation and addiction (*Lou, Anthea, Maud, Matt, Lucy, Candice, Alastair*). Studies consistently demonstrate that adverse childhood experiences (ACEs) such as CSA can have a significant impact on mental as well as physical health. Most notable is the link between ACEs and addiction, wherein individuals with four or more ACEs are seven times more likely to become addicted to alcohol, ten times more likely to be at risk of intravenous drug addiction and 12 times more likely to have attempted suicide (Felitti *et al.*, 1998).

Many survivors resort to alcohol or drugs from an early age to numb overwhelming emotions, escape from the horror of abuse and manage trauma symptoms such as flashbacks, intrusive memories, thoughts and feelings, or to counteract insomnia or avoid terrifying nightmares. Alcohol or drugs enable the survivor to escape being themselves by masking their self-loathing, shame and unlovability and pretending that they have not been affected by the abuse (Sanderson, 2019b). The use of alcohol and drugs becomes a form of self-medication (Khantzian, 1985; Maté, 2008). Survivors may not be aware that they are using alcohol or drugs to regulate their emotions, and may not be in touch with their abuse experiences until they have detoxed and are in recovery when suppressed memories and feelings return (Maté, 2008; Sanderson, 2019a).

As prolonged addiction is primarily caused by trauma and isolation, it can be seen as a signpost to earlier suffering and damaged attachments. It represents the struggle to survive and the search for attachment or a secure base, even if this can only be found in substances or process addictions. Thus, addiction becomes a form of attachment seeking and an adaptation to confused and frightening attachments in which dependency needs for human contact and attachment are transferred to dependency on their addiction (Flores, 2004; Gill, 2018).

In the absence of nurturing early environments that soothe or feel good, children learn to adapt to their environment and turn to other forms of relief, such as compulsive behaviours, or mood-altering substances like food, drugs and alcohol. In the absence of a safe and dependable attachment figure to turn to, the child is unable to regulate their emotions and comes to rely on substances that calm them or reduce the feeling of emptiness and despair by making them feel more (Sanderson, 2019a).

As relationships are seen as a source of danger rather than comfort, the addiction becomes the only trusted and consistent companion that is reliable and predictable. Over time, the addiction becomes the primary attachment and a substitute for the yearned-for connection. As the connection to others weakens, it reinforces the sense of isolation and aloneness, while increasing the need to numb the pain of loneliness (Flores, 2004).

Substance dependency can be seen as a flight from distress, making the painful more tolerable and life more liveable (Sanderson, 2019a, 2019b). The use of alcohol or drugs acts as an emotional anaesthetic to soothe and alter mood, and to regulate emotions and trauma reactions (Khantzian, 1985). Survivors who seek oblivion or to anaesthetize their pain will be drawn to opiates, such as heroin, morphine, cannabis, alcohol or prescription painkillers, to numb intense feelings of anger, rage and shame.

Survivors who are highly dissociative and shut down will prefer opiates that mimic dissociative states or process addictions that allow them to be immersed 'in the zone' or 'in the

bubble'. Alternatively, they will seek out stimulants to up-regulate their numbed state and make them feel more alive and
euphoric. They will be drawn to stimulants such as cocaine,
methamphetamine (crystal meth), ecstasy (MDMA), caffeine
or prescription drugs such as methylphenidate (Ritalin) to feel
more alert and alive, and counteract their sense of deadness.
Stimulants also act as a social lubricant to provide confidence
by suppressing feelings of shame and anxiety to facilitate connection and attachment (Sanderson, 2019a, 2019b).

Survivors who are highly dissociated and no longer register
feelings of pain or pleasure may resort to extreme stimulation
through process addictions which involve risky or thrill-seek-
ing behaviour, such as extreme sports, exposure to violence,
compulsive sexual behaviour or self-mutilation. This is due in
part to the mind and body shutting down all sensations and
only registering highly intense feelings that can penetrate the
dissociated state (Sanderson, 2019a). During these activities,
the release of endorphins and the feeling of euphoria can
become highly addictive. The surge of euphoria is akin to 'a
firework display', which energizes them, and helps them to feel
more confident and able to function better mentally. The sense
of feeling good and the increased 'liquid confidence' makes it
easier to connect to others, form attachments and experience
a sense of belongingness, and feel truly alive.

Thus, the drug of choice makes life more bearable, as it
either numbs the pain by inducing oblivion or promotes
euphoria, and a feeling of being alive. Self-medicating the pain
is a survival strategy to regulate emotions and mood, and is
often seen as a life saver as it helps them to bear the unbearable
(One in Four, 2019; Sanderson, 2019a).

Trauma reactions and mental health

Survivors of CSA commonly experience a range of trauma reactions, such as complex post-traumatic stress disorder and mental health problems. It is clear from the narratives that all of the survivors had experienced an erosion of mental well-being and mental health difficulties at various times in their lives, and that these were often not linked to the abuse by either the survivors themselves or professionals. Nearly all of the survivors suffered from a range of trauma reactions such as hyper- or hypoarousal, flashbacks (*Lou, Chris, Matt, Lucy*), nightmares, intrusive memories and dissociative symptoms (*Muriel, Lou, Anthea, Maud, Chris, Matt, Candice, Alastair*). Some survivors reported mental breakdowns (*Lou, Anthea*) with some being hospitalized (*Anthea*) and over-medicated (*Muriel*).

Some of the survivors suffered from depression (*Muriel, Chris, Matt, Alastair*), chronic anxiety (*Muriel, Chris, Alastair*), eating disorders (*Lou, Chris*), self-harm (*Matt*), self-sabotaging or risky behaviour (*Muriel, Lou*), while some were also diagnosed with psychosis (*Lou*) and paranoia (*Matt*). The lure of suicide resonated throughout the narratives as suicidal ideation and/or suicide attempts (*Lou, Maud, Matt, Candice*). As survivors of CSA often feel that a part of them died during the abuse, they often feel they have nothing left to live for, making suicide a captivating option. Some of the suicide attempts were overt, whereas others were more covert in courting death through playing Russian roulette by placing themselves in risky or dangerous situations, such as drinking to oblivion or taking enormous quantities of drugs (*Lou, Maud, Candice*). Death was often seen as the only option to permanently escape the pain of the CSA and the enslavement of the addiction.

Some survivors experienced emotional breakdowns (*Lou, Anthea*) and repeated hospitalizations (*Anthea*). When seeking help some survivors felt that professionals either did not link current difficulties with a history of CSA and trauma, or minimized or dismissed the CSA, and as a result were misdiagnosed or given inappropriate treatment interventions which delayed their healing and recovery.

Physical health problems

Many survivors described a range of health problems in which their physical health was compromised, leading to autoimmune disorders and a range of other health issues (*Lou, Anthea, Chris, Lucy, Samia*). These were often exacerbated by sleep disturbances and recurring nightmares (*Muriel*).

Survivors can also feel a sense of body betrayal due to somatization in which they experience a range of unexplained chronic illnesses such as pelvic and genital pain, irritable bowel syndrome and other hyper-immune disorders including recurring allergies and skin conditions. Some survivors experience excruciating muscle pain, or intense physical or mental exhaustion commonly associated with chronic fatigue syndrome or sleep problems such as chronic insomnia (Sanderson, 2015, 2019; van der Kolk, 2015).

Isolation and loneliness

The fear and terror experienced by survivors means that they are unable to trust others, let alone themselves. Alongside this, shame and needing to keep the secret means that may survivors withdraw from others. This leads to self-imposed isolation, loneliness, inability to socialize and fear of intimacy and relationships (*Anthea, Maud, Matt, Alastair*). This results in not being able to live fully, living in their heads while cut off from their bodies, with a lack of spontaneity and ability to engage in the world.

Losses

Common losses associated with CSA include actual and symbolic losses such as loss of childhood, loss of protective parent(s), loss of a nurturing family, as well as the loss of self. Loss of trust in self and others as well as loss of belief that the world can be a benign place are also common. In addition, they report a loss of stability and certainty, the loss of mental and physical health, and the loss of a sense of self (*Lou, Anthea, Maud, Chris, Matt, Samia, Alastair*). Many of our survivors described being robbed of self-worth, self-respect, self-belief and self-esteem, and experiencing a loss of control and autonomy.

Many survivors felt that their childhood and sexuality had been stolen along with opportunities to have stable relationships and children and families of their own (*Lou, Maud, Matt*), as they had a fear of parenting (*Lucy*).

Some survivors mourned the loss of well-being, loss of control over their body, loss of continuity or belongingness, loss of healthy relationships and the belief in a better future in which they could experience inner peace or contentment. Spiritual losses cluster around loss of faith and, in the case of clerical abuse, loss of belief in their faith. With regard to current and future losses survivors mourn the loss of not being able to give voice to their lived experience (*Maud*) alongside the loss of hope in restoring damaged family relationships or the yearned-for relationship with the abuser(s) or non-abusing parent(s) as well as educational and vocational opportunities.

Seeking help

The lack of understanding of the impact of CSA and limited access to specialist services means that many survivors are misdiagnosed or referred to unhelpful counselling which often makes them feel more vulnerable. Some survivors reported that professionals were often not able to link behaviour and presenting symptoms to a history of CSA and lacked understanding and knowledge about the impact of sexual abuse (*Anthea, Chris, Samia*) or felt dismissed or minimized (*Candice*). Conversely, those survivors who felt heard and understood by professionals found that they were able gradually to heal and recover from their abuse (*Muriel, Lou, Maud, Matt*), as were those who found community and a sense of belonging through the 12-Step Programme (*Lou, Matt*).

Difficulties when seeking help is a common theme for many survivors, whether it is from professionals such as social workers, GPs or counsellors. Many survivors feel let down and disappointed when first seeking help as many professionals fail to identify the abuse or are unable to link behaviour and symptoms to CSA. In seeking therapeutic help, survivors are often initially referred to generic, short-term therapy with counsellors who have little or no understanding of, or specialist training in, CSA. This means that they are not only misunderstood, but often misdiagnosed, stigmatized and in some cases over-medicated. As a result, many survivors face years of ineffective therapy which make some feel more vulnerable and damaged, often blaming themselves for the lack of therapeutic success. Many survivors desperately seek therapeutic support, sometimes innumerable times with different therapists and types of therapy, in the hope of finding much needed specialist help (One in Four, 2015, 2019; Sanderson, 2013a).

Many survivors find that specialist trauma-focused therapy

is most helpful, as they can break the silence and secrecy of CSA in a non-judgemental environment, feel seen, heard and understood and can reduce the crippling sense of shame. In addition, being able to feel and express their needs and suppressed feelings of anger and sadness is a key element to healing and allows them to re-connect to self and others, reclaim their sense of self and restore relational worth (see Chapter 3).

Practitioner narratives

The common themes that emerged from the participants who wrote from a practitioner perspective illustrate the need for survivors to have a voice and to be believed in a safe therapeutic space that is non-shaming and bears witness to the legacy of CSA.

Most practitioners referred to the use of trauma-informed practice in understanding trauma reactions, and the need to adopt a trauma-informed perspective which highlights the importance of safety and trustworthiness and identifies triggers that activate trauma reactions such as media coverage of CSA, childbirth and becoming parents. They highlighted the need for stabilization to facilitate emotional regulation through the use of self-care strategies and grounding techniques, including mindfulness and somatic safety. Practitioners also acknowledged the importance of psychoeducation around trauma, dissociation, the trauma bond, shame and self-blame, and understanding symptoms as protective survival strategies.

There was a recognition (*Maria, Reena*) that the misuse of power and control in CSA results in powerlessness and helplessness and that it is imperative to ensure that power and control dynamics are not replicated in the therapeutic relationship. In focusing on empowering the survivor, practitioners are able to restore a sense of control, self-agency and opportunity to reclaim their authentic self. Some practitioners (*Reena, Willis*) alluded to the need for clinicians to have an understanding of the impact of transgenerational trauma, including racism and marginalization, and how survivors bear the legacy of such trauma, and the need for practitioners to be aware of how these intersect.

All the practitioner narratives highlighted the need to adopt a relational and attachment focus involving relational depth and contact, in which to restore authentic relations and self-worth. To facilitate this, practitioners need to be emotionally available to counteract lack of emotional availability in childhood, and to offer constancy and consistency. It is through such a therapeutic relationship that survivors can access and express their needs, suppressed feelings such as sadness and rage, and restore trust in self and others. This will enable them to set healthy boundaries, learn new ways of relating and new relationship skills, and build resilience. To enhance the quality of the therapeutic relationships, it is essential that practitioners practise reflexivity and self-reflection and are aware of their own needs and vulnerability (*Willis*) to truly connect and cultivate relational depth.

The survivor narratives provide powerful indices of what survivors need therapeutically, while the practitioner narratives mirror what are considered to be essential principles of the Power Threat Meaning Framework (Johnstone & Boyle, 2018), trauma-informed practice and an attachment and relational approach, which are the focus of the next chapter.

CHAPTER 3

What Survivors Tell Us They Need to Heal

Not only are the themes in these narratives fundamental to our understanding of survivors of CSA, they also provide a wealth of data to help clinicians become more aware of the impact of CSA and what needs to be processed therapeutically. They also highlight the power and control dynamics that practitioners need to be mindful of to ensure that these are not replicated in the therapeutic process, in order to reduce the risk of re-traumatization.

These narratives, alongside others, have given survivors an opportunity to express what it is they need to help them heal (Independent Inquiry into Child Sexual Abuse, 2017; One in Four, 2015, 2019; Smith, Dogaru & Ellis, 2015). In combination, these consistently iterate that survivors need to be heard through giving voice to what happened to them, without feeling judged or shamed. They also need to be seen as experts on their lived experience, and treated as equal participants in the therapeutic process.

This requires therapists to equalize the power and control dynamics in the therapeutic relationship and ensure that survivors are given autonomy to make their own choices and are empowered throughout the therapeutic process to fully achieve personal growth. This is best achieved through a non-hierarchical and collaborative approach based on mutuality and respect. Survivors need to know that the practitioner is professional, trustworthy and practises ethically. In order to feel safe, practitioners need to be able to hold appropriate boundaries, be emotionally well regulated, reflective and engage in regular supervision. Survivors also need to know that practitioners have processed their own experiences and do not contaminate the therapeutic space with their own unprocessed memories and past emotions.

Many survivors report the benefits of having access to specialist, longer-term trauma therapy that processes the trauma at a pace that is manageable rather than them being rushed through short-term or time-restricted therapy. Survivors also report that support from therapists who had specialist training or expertise in working with survivors of CSA, who were trauma aware and who genuinely cared, were the most effective in enabling survivors to connect to themselves and others (One in Four, 2015, 2019). It is this, alongside a relational approach to restore relational worth, that allows survivors to break the cycle of abuse, find their voice and learn to live again.

Some survivors also find that support from family and friends and other survivors through group therapy or psycho-educational workshops provides them with a sense of belonging and is also highly beneficial in their journey to recovery and healing (One in Four, 2015, 2019). Many survivors report that a range of therapeutic modalities is helpful, including somatic therapy, EMDR, expressive therapies, group work and the 12-Step Programme for those survivors who have a prolonged history of addiction (One in Four, 2019). Many survivors express the need for an awareness of the power and control imbalance in the therapeutic relationship and the capacity to see trauma through the eyes of each individual survivor rather than relying on theory or research.

With regard to therapeutic interventions, survivors feel that a number of healing strategies are beneficial, including grounding techniques, meditation, reconnecting to the body, regular exercise, reading self-help books, personal development workshops, self-awareness, self-love, self-care and having a creative outlet through art and performance, especially music or singing. The most powerful source of healing is felt to be connecting with and developing friendships and building a support network with others, including other survivors, to break the silence and alleviate the sense of shame (One in Four, 2015, 2019).

Much of what survivors tell us they need is echoed by the narratives of the practitioners in this work, all of whom emphasized the need for an attachment-focused approach which is based on relational depth and warmth. Much of what the survivors' and practitioners' narratives tell us is incorporated into the Power Threat Meaning Framework, the fundamental principles of trauma-informed practice and the phased-oriented approach to trauma therapy. To help professionals working with survivors become trauma-wise practitioners, they need to familiarize themselves with these approaches and integrate them into their preferred modality. This does not mean abandoning their practice model, but rather using them as a scaffold to their modality and incorporating many of the factors that survivors have identified as being helpful in their healing and recovery. If practitioners adopt these, survivors will feel more understood, held and truly empowered to reclaim their lives.

Therapeutic practice

When working with survivors of CSA and complex trauma it is essential to have an understanding of the impact of power and control dynamics inherent in abuse. Survivors of CSA will have experienced abuse by people who had authority and power over them which they could not challenge. To survive such power and control, survivors will have learnt to become compliant and submissive, and feel they have little or no sense of self-agency or freedom to make autonomous choices. With that in mind, trauma-wise practitioners need to be aware of the impact of power and control on survivors and ensure that they provide a secure and safe therapeutic space in which trauma is seen through the eyes of each individual survivor. In addition, practitioners need to ensure that power dynamics are equalized and survivors are offered choices and encouraged to be active agents in their healing, and that the therapist is a reliable and faithful companion on their journey to recovery.

This entails creating both physical as well as emotional safety, trustworthiness and collaboration, and providing choices in order to empower clients. Due to the myriad of betrayals by authority figures experienced by survivors, it is critical that practitioners are experienced as trustworthy, and that this is consistently conveyed to, as well as felt by, the survivor (Butler, Critelli & Rinfrette, 2011). This can be effected by being explicit in terms of boundaries, managing expectations, articulating therapist and client responsibilities and respecting clients' emotional limits and not judging them when they feel overwhelmed or stuck and unable to fully engage in the work. Practitioners need to ensure that they do not shame clients by interpreting their behaviour as resistant but rather understand it as a protective survival strategy that has been activated as a result of fear or shame.

The Power Threat Meaning Framework

When working with complex trauma in which there has been an abuse of power, practitioners may benefit from viewing emotional distress and concomitant behaviours not just as symptoms but within the context of the person's experiences, and their attempts at making sense of these. To this effect, Johnstone and Boyle's Power Threat Meaning Framework (Boyle & Johnstone, 2020; Johnstone & Boyle, 2018). proposes an alternative approach to traditional models based on psychiatric diagnosis and the primary focus on symptoms. The emphasis in the Power Threat Meaning Framework is to understand *what has happened* to the person rather than *what is wrong with* them. It is a way of understanding how people try to make sense of difficult and confusing experiences in order to gain meaning. Furthermore, it locates the emotional distress and concomitant behaviours as responses, or adaptations, to being controlled and subjected to the misuse of power. Practitioners need to ensure that they do not re-traumatize survivors by validating their narratives, and link their responses to their abuse experiences rather than pathologize or shame them for their 'symptoms'. Through making the link between distress and the abuse of power, survivors can begin to reclaim their power and control.

With this in mind, practitioners need to structure their approach in encouraging survivors to tell their story and focus on asking what has happened to them and how this affected them, to get a sense of how power was used to control them and what threats this posed. In addition, it is essential to explore what sense they made of their experiences and the meaning they have ascribed to these. Alongside this, practitioners need to help survivors, without judgement, to identify their threat responses and what they had to do to survive, and to recognize which ones they are still currently using. This includes contextualizing and understanding behaviours and responses that appear to be counter-therapeutic as protective survival strategies rather than non-compliant, resistant or avoidant (Boyle & Johnstone, 2020; Sanderson, 2015b).

In order to manage power dynamics ethically, it is essential to reduce the intrinsic structural power in the therapeutic encounter by acknowledging and discussing power dynamics and the rights and responsibilities of both parties. This needs to be supported by a sharing of power and knowledge through psychoeducation and promoting equality, autonomy, agency and choice to mitigate reinforcing powerlessness and helplessness. Alongside sharing power, practitioners must be able to modulate control dynamics by encouraging survivors to take control in their lives as well as the therapeutic space, and be willing to relinquish control by not being too directive or expecting clients to work at a pace that suits them rather than what is manageable.

To ensure that survivors feel safe, practitioners need to promote choices in where the survivor sits, the positioning of the chairs, and the physical space between practitioner and client. Survivors need to be able to see the door and feel that they have a choice in how closely the chairs are positioned, and at which angle. Many survivors feel uncomfortable sitting directly opposite the practitioner as this may replicate the scrutiny of the abuser during the abuse, and may feel more comfortable if the chairs are placed at an angle, or side by side, at least initially. This also helps to regulate eye contact as it is often under the gaze of others that shame is induced, and trauma-wise practitioners need to be mindful that the intensity of eye gaze, and eye contact, can be triggering and lead to dissociation. Trauma-wise practitioners are encouraged to share the regulation of this with each client to find the optimal distance that feels safe for them.

In addition, survivors need to feel that they have a choice in whether to talk or not to talk, and to find a way of regulating silence. While therapeutic silences can be very fruitful opportunities to reflect and access feelings, for many survivors silence is experienced as punitive and is reminiscent of the abuse. It is essential that practitioners regulate the silence appropriately, and that prolonged silences do not trigger or activate shamed or dissociative states. The shame associated with CSA is easily evoked, and when it is accompanied by prolonged silence, survivors may interpret this as judgement, rejection and abandonment.

Many of the tenets in the Power Threat Meaning Framework are reflected in the core principles of trauma-informed practice in which the focus is also on what happened to the survivor rather than pathologizing them (Fallot & Harris, 2008; Quiros & Berger, 2015), particularly the need for safety, trustworthiness, collaboration, choice and empowerment.

Trauma-informed practice

Whichever type of treatment option is accessed, it is important that it is regulated and sensitively paced so that the survivor is not re-traumatized. This is best achieved through a phased-oriented approach using the principles of trauma-informed practice (Herman, 2001; Rothschild, 2017; Sanderson, 2022) which can be incorporated within a particular treatment approach. The advantage of employing the principles of trauma-informed practice is that survivors can go at their own pace, and can cultivate the necessary resources to enable them to explore the trauma without becoming re-traumatized, and develop skills that will enable them to become more resilient and allow for post-traumatic growth.

The core principles of trauma-informed practice are: safety, trustworthiness, choice, collaboration and empowerment (Fallot & Harris, 2008; Quiros & Berger, 2015; Sanderson, 2022). These need to be accompanied by an awareness of trauma and its impact and the ability to look at trauma through the eyes of each individual. The focus is on creating safety and trust, and the opportunity to work collaboratively while offering choices and respecting autonomy. It also identifies the individual's strengths, and emphasizes that recovery from trauma is possible and that there is hope (Elliott *et al.*, 2005).

Equalizing and sharing of power is crucial in order to enable empowerment. This is facilitated through collaboration in which the survivor is accorded respect and seen as an expert on their own life and experiences (Elliott *et al.*, 2005). Alongside collaboration, trauma-wise practitioners need to ensure that they respect a client's right to make autonomous choices, for example in the type of treatment modality, intervention, planning and evaluation of treatment, and that they provide the opportunity to restore control and build trust in self-reliance.

Most importantly, practitioners need to recognize and validate the resources and skills that survivors already have that have enabled them to survive, including courage and resilience. If the focus is on the survivor's strength, they will feel empowered by their strategies for survival rather than rendered helpless. This can lay the foundation for further empowerment during the therapeutic process in the acquisition of more skills and the reclaiming of control over their body, and mind and future (Butler *et al.*, 2011).

Throughout the therapeutic process, practitioners need to view trauma through the eyes of each individual survivor and hold a position of hope that recovery is possible, especially when survivors become disconsolate or despondent.

Phased-oriented trauma therapy

Trauma-informed practice can be aided by adopting a phased-oriented approach to working with trauma (Baranowsky & Gentry, 2014; Zaleski, Johnson & Klein, 2016). This trauma-focused treatment can be combined in a single specialist approach or incorporated into any existing modality or practice. The model consists of four phases: stabilization, processing, integration and justice. While these are four distinct phases, clinicians and survivors need to be aware that they are not linear and that survivors can oscillate between phases and there will be diversions, distractions and – at times – increased distress.

The movement between phases is fluid and is determined by the survivor's readiness to move to the next phase, rather than the length of time in each phase. It is also dependent on the mastery of the skills in each phase. If clients become too overwhelmed in Phase II, they can return to Phase I to acquire and master more grounding skills.

Some survivors may not be able to move beyond Phase I and practitioners need to accept that as it may be sufficient to significantly improve the management of trauma reactions and emotional regulation without being catapulted back into the traumatic past. Practitioners need to guard against being too rigid and prescriptive and acknowledge that healing is not about remembering or recalling all past experiences (van der Kolk, 2015) – van der Kolk argues that remembering is not the road to recovery and that survivors can be resourced to manage trauma reactions through grounding techniques and increasing distress tolerance, which minimizes the risk of being catapulted back into the past when triggered.

Some of the components in the stabilization phase, such as psychoeducation and grounding skills, can be delivered as group workshops, from which survivors can progress into one-to-one sessions. Many survivors report that group work that emphasizes raising awareness and understanding of CSA is an invaluable source of support which helps them make sense of their abuse experiences and enables them to link symptoms, trauma reactions and current behaviours to their CSA experiences.

Table 1: The phased-oriented approach to trauma recovery (adapted from Herman, 2001, 2023)

Phase I: Stabilization	Phase II: Processing	Phase III: Integration	Phase IV: Justice
Safety, grounding, resources, psychoeducation	Processing the trauma experiences	Make meaning, building resilience, reconnection	Apology, restorative justice

Phase I: Stabilization

The focus here is on creating safety, promoting self-care, improving daily life, identifying the survivor's strengths and coping strategies, and assessing their current needs. During this phase, emphasis is placed on developing stabilization skills, such as grounding and emotional self-regulation in order to manage overwhelming trauma reactions, and building a personalized recovery toolkit.

Identifying and building resources

The first step in healing and recovery is to establish a good support network and make a list of their contact details. This should include professionals such as the doctor and social worker, as well as useful organizations and trusted friends or family members.

To maximize the building of resources, it is crucial to take stock of the existing resources that have enabled the individual to survive, by recording their strengths and existing resources. This enables them to feel less powerless and to find ways in which these can aid their recovery. These resources can also be cultivated with the introduction of new skills such as grounding strategies and mindfulness. It is helpful to find a way of noting down resources that work, either in a journal or workbook, or on a smartphone so they are easily accessible, as they form the basis of their recovery toolkit.

Psychoeducation

Psychoeducation is crucial in understanding how the body reacts to distress and in making sense of how trauma impacts on the mind and body. It also helps the survivor to make the link between CSA and emotional self-regulation. This, alongside the stabilization skills, will enable them to learn more adaptive skills to regulate their emotional reactions and tolerate distress when exploring memories of CSA.

Reframing symptoms as survival strategies (which are now no longer needed) or as the source of difficulties allows the survivor to have a better understanding of their behaviours. Psychoeducation also empowers the survivor to regain a sense of control and reduces shame and self-blame, which is necessary to develop compassion and empathy for the self and what has happened to them.

Emotional self-regulation

Learning new skills for emotional self-regulation to help the survivor stay in their window of tolerance is best achieved through healthy, healing relationships and with consistent practice. It is helpful to build relaxation and distress tolerance techniques into every session.

These techniques can include regular exercise to discharge trapped energy, adrenaline and distress hormones, or relaxation and mindfulness skills that pay attention to body sensations and increase physical awareness.

Trigger inventory

In order to feel more in control of trauma reactions and emotional dysregulation it is helpful to make a list of triggers that set off the emotional alarm system, such as specific situations, sensations, people, places and feelings that lead to emotional dysregulation. In knowing the triggers that activate trauma reactions, survivors are forewarned and can put emotional self-regulation skills in place. Recognizing and identifying emotions can help the survivor to make an inventory of the triggers that induce dissociative states and shame, and implement grounding techniques such as breathing and self-soothing skills that increase the tolerance of distress and help to calm and regulate overwhelming reactions.

Grounding techniques

An important tool in helping to ground survivors is to encourage them to focus their attention on the present by asking them to concentrate on the physical space around them and identify and name out loud three objects or colours in their surrounding environment. This can be used in any indoor or outdoor space and is a good technique before and after each session to manage difficult feelings.

It also helps to ask them to notice sensory stimuli in their external environment, such as the rustling of leaves, the sun, rain or wind on the skin, the smell of flowers, or the sound of birdsong.

Anchors

To help survivors feel more anchored in the present it is useful to find an object (pebble, crystal, favourite scarf or pen) that is portable and which they have with them at all times (a ring, other pieces of jewellery, watch, handkerchief) that they can touch or hold and use to ground themselves and remind them to breathe. This can be accompanied by identifying three objects in any one room and focusing on these whenever they feel anxious or emotionally overwhelmed, or start to dissociate. This can be extended to other places, such as work, college, car or public spaces. It is worth keeping a record of the ones that are most effective in a journal or smartphone so they are easily accessible whenever things are difficult.

Safe place

In addition, it can be helpful to identify a safe place that survivors can retreat to when feeling overwhelmed. This might also include activities that promote relaxation, such as having a warm bath, massage, meditation, sitting in the sunshine in the park, reading, watching a film, listening to music, going to a concert or watching or playing sport. Some survivors find it uncomfortable to relax and may prefer invigorating activities that are a source of pleasure, such as swimming, exercising, playing sports, dancing, singing, going for a walk or running.

A safe place can be from the past or present, which has

been or is a source of safety, but survivors who have never experienced a safe place will need to imagine one. This could be sitting on a beach, in a tree house, a garden, or mountain walk. Whether this is real or imagined, it is helpful to include as many sensory cues as possible to the safe place to maximize the grounding effect.

Grounding skills

The most effective way to regulate emotional states is through grounding using all the five senses: sight, sound, touch, smell and taste. These can be used to calm and soothe (down-regulate) when feeling overwhelmed and hyperaroused, or to stimulate (up-regulate) when dissociated or hypoaroused. There are a range of grounding skills that make use of sensory stimuli, the body, the mind and creativity that the survivors can explore to find what is most effective for them and essential tools for their recovery toolkit (see Table 2, below). It is important to allow each survivor to identify what works for them rather than being prescriptive, and ensure that they practise and rehearse these so that they become automatic, alternative responses to emotional dysregulation.

Grounding skills can help survivors to reconnect and orient themselves to the present by anchoring them in their body and sensations, through all the sensory channels. This can include movement through dancing, walking, exercise, shifting position, posture, feet on floor, or star jumps. Regulating through touch can be through massage, wrapping up in a blanket, feeling sunlight or air on the skin, having a warm or cold bath or shower or baking, knitting or making pottery. Being in touch with auditory sensations can include enjoying quiet moments, listening to music, birdsong, rain, water or wind rustling, or whistling, humming or singing.

Some survivors prefer visual stimuli to help ground them, such as looking at favourite photos, paintings, the sunset or sunrise, a fire, cloud formations or seeing a film. Smell can have a powerful impact on mood and can be enhanced by scented candles, essential oils, perfume, baking, flowers or herbal tea. Many survivors find that chewing something crunchy or strongly flavoured such as chilli or lemon can ground them if they have dissociated, or a warm drink can soothe them if they feel overwhelmed.

Table 2: Grounding skills

Senses	Smell – essential oil, herbal tea bag, scent, spices, scented candle
	Taste – honey, sweet tea (soothing), chilli, lemon (stimulting)
	Sound – music (energizing or soothing), birdsong, water
	Touch – soft toy, blanket, silk or woollen scarf, ice
	Visual – grounding image, photo, painting, screensaver
Body	Breathing – blow bubbles, blow up balloon
	Body position – favourite blanket, stand up straight, clench and release muscle tension
	Body in action – walk, exercise, sport, dance, movement, pull a funny face, yoga, martial arts
	Voice – grounding phrase, grounding song, sing, recite a poem, shout, laugh
Mind	Refocus attention – identify three objects/colours in the room, notice the rustling of leaves, the feeling of sun on skin, the smell of flowers, sound of birdsong, stress or juggling balls, tangle toys
	Reorient in time – date, time, note differences between today and past
	Distraction – count back from 100 in threes, Sudoku, puzzles, colouring books

cont.

Creativity	Arts – paint, draw, make pottery, sculpt, play musical instrument, write song or poem
	Create – bake, cook, garden, knit, build something
	Immersion – grounding hobby
Containment	Box or container – place worries, shame, negative thoughts, fears inside the box
	Balloon – place concerns inside balloon and let go

Mood basket

A mood basket or mood box is another way to regulate feelings and mood. While a basket is useful as it can be easily transported between rooms or locations, a box with a lock will ensure greater privacy. The idea is to place things that are calming, grounding or inspirational into the basket or box so that they are easily accessible. These can include calming images, cards or postcards, meaningful pebbles, stones, crystals, favourite photographs or flowers. Other items could include a favourite book, poem or quotation, a piece of music, a calming scent or aroma, or objects from a time or place associated with good memories, jewellery from a loved one, a piece of cloth or a soft toy, and a favourite treat or healthy snack. Whenever the survivor feels overwhelmed or despondent they can take something from the mood basket to ground themselves.

It can also help to make a relaxation kit containing items such as a scented candle, a favourite sweater, shawl, socks, blanket or comforter, which is easy to access whenever the survivor needs to relax and nurture themselves.

Breathing

To help reduce anxiety and overwhelming emotion it is important to be able to breathe effectively. A common response to anxiety and fear is to breathe too quickly or shallowly, thereby reducing the amount of oxygen in the body. As a result, the body begins to panic, which trips the alarm system and heightens physical and psychological arousal and fear responses. The lack of oxygen also causes dizziness and shakiness, which only serves to increase the panic.

Mindfulness

An invaluable aid to grounding and becoming more alert and able to focus is mindfulness. It helps to calm the mind and access a more peaceful, relaxed state of awareness. Most importantly, it helps to tolerate and reduce difficult, painful or frightening thoughts, feelings and sensations. In practising mindfulness, survivors are able to gain a sense of mastery over thoughts and feelings, rather than being controlled by them.

Mindfulness essentially means coming back into awareness, or coming back into the present moment. It is a way of becoming more present and embodied, which is often difficult for survivors who have a terror of inner experiencing and whose body has betrayed them.

Mindfulness can be practised in many different ways, and not always through closing the eyes, or sitting still. It can be practised at any time, including when the body is active, for example doing yoga, dancing or walking. The essential thing is to notice what is happening both internally and externally.

Mindfulness while moving can sometimes be more beneficial for survivors who are dissociative, as sitting still and focusing on inner experiencing can catapult them into a dissociative state, which is the antithesis of mindfulness.

As many survivors are fearful of being in their body, it is important to incorporate trauma-safe adjustments when practising mindfulness. Rothschild (2017) proposes that combining interoception (sensing internal signals from the body) with exteroception (sensation that results from stimuli located outside the body which are detected through vision, hearing, smell, touch or taste) feels safer for some clients as it allows for dual awareness of both internal and external stimuli, and prevents becoming too immersed in the body. In addition it is important to reduce initial exposure to mindfulness, such as 60 seconds rather than 10–15 minutes, to allow flexibility with regard to sitting, standing or walking, and to keep eyes open rather than closing them.

As mentioned above, it is often more helpful to start with 60-second mindfulness exercises and build up from this. It is important that survivors can choose to keep their eyes open, as closing the eyes may be triggering and can activate the alarm system and lead to dissociation. Survivors need to know that they can vary the way they practise mindfulness to suit their own needs, and that the emphasis is on noticing rather than judging or evaluating. Rather than meditation or the relaxation technique, which can be triggering, it may be better to start off with progressive muscular relaxation, which involves the tensing and relaxing of various muscle groups to allow the survivor to feel more in control over their body rather than entering a dissociative state.

The most important thing is to help the survivor experiment with a mixture of techniques rather than prescribing a single one. This will allow them to discover the techniques that work best for them, so that they are more able to regulate their emotions and reduce the risk of self-harm.

Some of the components in the stabilization phase, such as psychoeducation and grounding skills, can be delivered as group workshops, from which survivors can progress to one-to-one sessions. Many survivors report that group work which emphasizes raising awareness and understanding CSA is an invaluable source of support that helps them make sense of their abuse experiences and the link to current behaviour.

Phase II: Processing

Once the survivor has mastered stabilization skills and established a wider window of tolerance, they can enter Phase II, where the focus is on processing the CSA. This includes processing the trauma experiences and managing flashbacks, nightmares and unprocessed memories. In processing these, survivors can integrate memories into a coherent narrative and begin to develop a more adaptive and cohesive sense of self and others. Throughout this processing, survivors can begin to realize the harm done and become aware of distorted perceptions of self, others and the world, which can be challenged to restore their trust and self-belief. In addition, they can begin to reallocate shame and responsibility, and grieve the many losses associated with CSA. In releasing the pain and sorrow, they can begin to feel empathy and self-compassion for the child that was hurt and betrayed. This allows them to reappraise unresolved traumatic memories and begin to restore reality by identifying the deception and distortion of reality which lead to self-blame, guilt and shame. In addition, they can process suppressed feelings such as rage and sadness and work through the recurring themes of self-blame, guilt, shame, loss, compromised sexuality, and parenting fears.

Clinicians must make sure that the processing phase is appropriately paced so that the survivor is neither rushed nor becomes too focused on recovering memories and details of the abuse, as these may lead to desensitization and numbing rather than integration. The emphasis is not on remembering every detail of the abuse but on making links and being able to love in the present without being catapulted back into the past (Sanderson, 2022; van der Kolk, 2015).

Phase III: Integration

This phase aims to consolidate the skills learnt in Phases I and II and begin to integrate the abuse experiences. In reclaiming reality, survivors can start to make more sense of their experiences and build meaning. In reconnecting to the self like this, they can begin to feel empathy and compassion for themselves and, in accepting themselves, develop greater trust in themselves and others. In reconnecting to others and the world they can build and rebuild relationships, and re-engage with life and their community, as well as educational, occupational and vocational choices. This is also the time to reclaim their spirituality, build resilience and embrace authentic pride.

In letting go of shame and focusing on self-acceptance, survivors can build authentic pride. Through self-empathy and acceptance, they can release the internalized anger and rage that has been directed against themselves and can begin to reclaim and acknowledge their achievements and accomplishments to build authentic pride.

This can be aided by encouraging them to make a list of their achievements and sources of authentic pride, no matter how minimal or undervalued these are by the survivor. These can be written on post-it notes, which can be folded into small squares and placed into a jar. Whenever the survivor needs to remind themselves of their value and worth they can take out one of the notes from the 'cookie jar' and, in reading it, allow themselves to feel a resurgence of authentic pride.

This paves the way for post-traumatic growth, in which the survivor is able to reconnect to the self, others and the world.

Phase IV: Justice

This phase focuses on the importance of justice to allow survivors to fully heal. This includes restorative justice, apology and recognition from the larger community that harm has been done, along with empathy and compassion for those who have been harmed. In addition, those who have been directly or indirectly complicit in the abuse such as indifferent bystanders, institutions or the criminal justice system must be held accountable for secondary traumatization through stigmatization, not being believed or blamed. Such justice is essential in reducing shame and self-blame and is the only way to minimize marginalization and promote justice for all (Herman, 2023). Phase IV: Justice

This phase focuses on the importance of justice to allow survivors to fully heal. This includes restorative justice, apology and recognition from the larger community that harm has been done, along with empathy and compassion for those who have been harmed. In addition, those who have been directly or indirectly complicit in the abuse such as indifferent bystanders, institutions or the criminal justice system must be held accountable for secondary traumatization through stigmatization, not being believed or blamed. Such justice is essential in reducing shame and self-blame and is the only way to minimize marginalization and promote justice for all (Herman, 2023).

Post-traumatic growth

Giving survivors a voice and listening to their story is the first step in the process of healing, and with the right support survivors can rebuild their lives and enter the process of post-traumatic growth. In this process, they will develop a deeper sense of self and personal strengths, regain meaning and purpose, and have a greater appreciation of life.

Post-traumatic growth will allow survivors to become more open to new possibilities in life free from shame, in which they are able to reconnect to self, others and the world. This will help them to build relationships, get closer to others and feel more alive, which is transformative, not just for the survivor but also for all those who support them.

The power of a healing relationship

Testament to the survivor and practitioner narratives, healing and recovery are to be found in connection and forming healthy relationships that can accept the whole person rather than focusing on their identity as a survivor. It is crucial for practitioners to build a healing relationship in which the survivor feels safe and trusts sufficiently to break the silence and explore their CSA in more depth, without fear of further abuse or shame.

In the presence of a warm, compassionate and genuinely caring relationship, survivors can learn new ways of relating to others through setting healthy boundaries and developing more-effective communication skills. It also helps them to build mutual respect, enhance communication and develop relationship skills. This is a powerful antidote to their experience of relationships as a source of danger rather than a source of security, warmth and growth (Miller, 2015). Through this, the survivor can begin to enjoy their relationships rather than fearing shame, rejection or abandonment. This can transform their view of themselves and what it means to be connected, and they can feel the empowerment of post-traumatic growth.

The therapeutic relationship is fundamental to restoring

relational worth and aiding healing. It is also an opportunity for the survivor to experience new ways of relating and relationship skills which they can use to build or rebuild relationships with others, including family members. To undo the effects of CSA, it is crucial that practitioners are able to offer a genuinely warm, human relationship in which the survivor is valued and respected (Jordan, 2017).

To achieve this it is crucial to adopt a collaborative and non-hierarchical approach in which the survivor is able to take equal control of their healing rather than being controlled and directed by the therapist or the rigid adoption of the therapeutic modality (Sanderson, 2022). Trauma-wise practitioners need to be non-coercive, flexible and pace the work within limits that are manageable for the survivor (Sanderson, 2019a). This necessitates establishing a supportive, non-judgemental, non-shaming and sensitively attuned therapeutic relationship in which the survivor feels safe and respected.

Practitioners need to be emotionally available and attuned to the survivor and be fully engaged as a detached, blank screen approach is often experienced as re-traumatizing. The emphasis needs to be on being able to *be with* the survivor rather than *doing to them*. Thus it is vital to create a collaborative working alliance in which shared agreements are made about the expectations of both parties, and how these can be managed, along with relational safety, especially as the therapeutic relationship unfolds and grows. Alongside this, practitioners need to be clear and explicit in their communication to reduce the need to 'mind read'. Survivors have learned to mind read in order to protect themselves, and in the presence of unclear or mixed messages will do so in the therapeutic relationship. Practitioners need to regularly check the quality of the

WE ARE STILL HERE

communication in terms of what is said, received and how that is interpreted.

In order for the therapeutic process to be truly empowering, agreements need to be bidirectional rather than imposed and controlled by either party, and be open to negotiation as the therapeutic relationship evolves. This includes the repairing of ruptures and the ability of the practitioner to acknowledge their responsibility in making errors, mis-attuned, insensitive or shaming reflections, and to apologize for these. As abusers rarely take responsibility for the abuse or apologize for harm done, it is critical for survivors to be in the presence of someone who can admit and apologize for harm done. This reduces the self-blame and shame that survivors invariably internalize in the absence of accountability.

To reduce power and control dynamics, practitioners are cautioned not to make assumptions and to offer reflections and thoughts as possibilities or hypotheses rather than prescriptive interpretations, to avoid invalidating the survivor's experiences (Cozolino, 2021).

Alongside this, it is prudent to have regular reviews of how the survivor feels about the therapeutic process, what meaning they are making, the quality of the connection, therapeutic goals, and to what extent these are being achieved. Through such open discussion, both the survivor and practitioner can stay on track and revise and renegotiate as necessary (Sanderson, 2022) to more effectively manage both client and practitioner expectations, and retain a realistic, positive and hopeful outcome.

Support for professionals

Listening to and supporting survivors can be extremely harrowing and challenging, and clinicians must ensure that they are supported in their work with appropriate training, supervision and mentoring. Research has shown that frontline professionals are impacted when working with people who experience trauma or CSA through vicarious traumatization or compassion fatigue (Sanderson, 2022).

To protect themselves from the negative impact of caring for others it is helpful for practitioners to develop an understanding and increased awareness of their own symptoms of burnout, vicarious traumatization, compassion fatigue and secondary traumatic stress. This will enable them to check-in regularly with their emotional and psychological well-being and to track levels of emotional and physical depletion in order to put strategies in place to manage these and prevent further decompensation. Saakvitne and Pearlman (1996) suggest that practitioners develop a personalized warning system which enables them to recognize and identify symptoms of burnout on a scale of 1 to 10 (with 10 being the worst they have ever felt about their work, empathy and compassion, and 1 the best). To facilitate this, practitioners can identify the top three physical, emotional and behavioural warning signs that indicate disruptions to their well-being, and when to implement effective strategies before symptoms worsen (Saakvitne & Pearlman, 1996).

Regular monitoring of personal and professional functioning ensures that practitioners are robust and resilient enough to manage the demands and challenges of working with clients without feeling diminished or depleted. This needs to be accompanied by a range of strategies that will recalibrate their physical, emotional and psychological well-being. To effect this, practitioners are encouraged to consider a range of self-care strategies and how these can be implemented during sessions, post-sessions and in their personal life. Skovholt and

Trotter-Mathison (2016) emphasize the need to focus on being a 'good enough counsellor' who is well bounded and able to manage both client and practitioner expectations. In addition, practitioners are encouraged to establish a consistent and reliable support network that includes regular supervision, peer supervision as well as positive and enriching interactions with colleagues and co-workers (Sanderson, 2022).

It is essential that practitioners implement work-related as well as personal self-care strategies in order to maintain a balance between professional identity and personal values throughout the caring process. To manage the demands of the work they need to ensure that the work remains meaningful and that they are able to set realistic goals (Sanderson, 2022). In addition, they need to be able to create a comfortable and safe work environment and have a sense of self-efficacy with regard to the number of clients on their caseload, the number of sessions per day, and the length of break between each client. For example, it can be helpful to schedule the most complex or demanding clients in a block either at the beginning or at the end of the week, or at a time of day when the practitioner is most alert, energized and focused (Skovholt and Trotter-Mathison, 2016).

Practitioners will also need to set appropriate boundaries for their clients and themselves, through setting limits, being able to say no without feeling guilty, working reasonable hours, taking regular breaks, and counterbalancing client work with other professional activities such as training, teaching, writing, research or promoting mental health through some form of activism. In addition, they need to ensure regular supervision and continuous professional development training to extend their knowledge and enhance their confidence (Sanderson, 2022).

There are a range of self-care skills that practitioners can employ both during sessions and immediately after sessions which can ensure that they stay grounded and present. During sessions, it is helpful to have an anchor in the room to ground themselves mentally as well as physically, and remain embodied. In addition, practitioners need to be able to be aware of the somatic impact in their body through body scans to check for any tension, or somatic reactions, and to monitor signs of somatic countertransference (Sanderson, 2022). In incorporating regular self-care strategies, practitioners will be able to remain embodied and present when working with survivors and be able to facilitate the survivors' healing and post-traumatic growth.

References

Baranowsky, A. & Gentry, J. E. (2014). *Trauma Practice: Tools for Stabilization and Recovery*. New York, NY: Hogrefe Publishing.

Batty, D. (2011). White girls seen as 'easy meat' by Pakistani rapists, says Jack Straw. *The Guardian* [online]. Available at: www.theguardian.com/world/2011/jan/08/jack-straw-white-girls-easy-meat [Accessed 31 July 2020]

Boyle, M. & Johnstone, L. (2020). *A Straight Talking Introduction to the Power Threat Meaning Framework: An Alternative to Psychiatric Diagnosis*. Ross-on-Wye: PCCS Books.

Butler, L. D., Critelli, F. M. & Rinfrette, E. S. (2011). Trauma-informed care and mental health. *Directions in Psychiatry*, 31(3), 197–212.

Cozolino, L. (2021). *The Development of a Therapist: Healing Others – Healing Self* (The Norton Series on Interpersonal Neurobiology). Kindle edition.

Crenshaw, K. W. (1994). 'Mapping the Margins. Intersectionality, Identity Politics, and Violence Against Women of Color.' In M. Albertson Fineman & R. Mykitiuk (eds) *The Public Nature of Private Violence*, pp.93–118. New York, NY: Routledge.

Department for Education (2017). *Child Exploitation: Definition and Guidance for Practitioners*. London: Department for Education.

Elliott, D. E., Bjelajac, P., Fallot, R. D., Markoff, L. S. & Reed, B. G. (2005). Trauma-informed or trauma-denied: Principles and implementation of trauma-informed services for women. *Journal of Community Psychology*, 33(4), 461–477.

Fallot, R. D. & Harris, M. (2008). Trauma-informed approaches to systems of care. *Trauma Psychology Newsletter*, 3(1), 6–7.

Felitti, V. J., Anda, R. F., Nordenberg, D., Williamson, D. F., Spitz, A. M., Edwards, V. & Marks, J. S. (1998). Relationship of childhood abuse and household dysfunction to many of the leading causes of death in adults: The Adverse Childhood Experiences (ACE) Study. *American Journal of Preventive Medicine*, 14(4), 245–258.

Flores, P. J. (2004). *Addiction as an Attachment Disorder*. New York, NY: Jason Aronson.

Gill, R. (2018). *Addictions from an Attachment Perspective: Do Broken Bonds and Early Trauma Lead to Addictive Behaviours?* London: Routledge.

Herman, J. L. (2001). *Trauma and Recovery*, 2nd edition. New York, NY: Basic Books.

Herman, J. L. (2023). *Truth and Repair: How Trauma Survivors Envision Justice*. New York, NY: Basic Books.

Home Office (2021). Police Recorded Crime and Outcomes Open Data Tables. [Online.] Available at: www.gov.uk/government/ statistics/ police-recorded-crime-open-data-tables

Independent Inquiry into Child Sexual Abuse (2017). *Victim and Survivor Voices from the Truth Project*. IICSA.

Johnstone, L. & Boyle, M. (*et al.*) (2018). *The Power Threat Meaning Framework: Towards the identification of patterns in emotional distress, unusual experiences and troubled or troubling behaviour, as an alternative to functional psychiatric diagnosis*. Leicester: British Psychological Society.

Jordan, J. V. (2017). Relational-cultural theory: The power of connection to transform our lives. *The Journal of Humanistic Counselling*, 56, 3.

Khantzian, E. J. (1985) The self-medication hypothesis of addictive disorders: Focus on heroin and cocaine dependence. *American Journal of Psychiatry*, 142(11), 1259–1264.

Maté, G. (2008). *In the Realm of Hungry Ghosts*. Toronto: Vintage Canada.

McCartan, K., Anning, A. & Qureshi, E. (2021). *The Impact of Sibling Sexual Abuse on Adults who were Harmed as Children*. Bristol: University of the West of England.

Menakem, R. (2017). *My Grandmother's Hands: Racialized Trauma and the Pathway to Mending Our Hearts and Bodies*. Las Vegas: Central Recovery Press.

Miller, J. B. (2015). *The Healing Connection: How Women Form Relationships in Therapy and in Life*. Boston, MA: Beacon Press.

Ministry of Justice (2012). *Prisoners' Childhood and Family Backgrounds*. London: Ministry of Justice.

Nathanson, D.L. (1992). *Shame and Pride: Affect, sex, and the birth of the self*. New York: W.W. Norton.

One in Four (2015). *Survivors' Voices: Breaking the silence on living with the impact of child sexual abuse in the family environment*. London: One in Four.

One in Four (2019). *Numbing the Pain: Survivors' voices of childhood sexual abuse and addiction*. London: One in Four.

Quiros, L. & Berger, R. (2015). Responding to the sociopolitical complexity of trauma: An integration of theory and practice. *Journal of Loss and Trauma*, 20(2), 149–159.

Rhodes, J. (2015). 'Prelude' in *Survivors' Voices: Breaking the silence on living with the impact of child sexual abuse in the family environment*. London: One in Four.

Rothschild, B. (2017). *The Body Remembers Volume 2: Revolutionizing Trauma Treatment*. New York, NY: W.W. Norton & Company.

Saad, L. (2020). *Me and White Supremacy: How to Recognise Your Privilege, Combat Racism and Change the World*. USA: SourceBooks.

Saakvitne, K. W. & Pearlman, L. A. (1996). *Transforming the Pain: A Workbook on Vicarious Traumatization*. New York, NY: W.W. Norton & Company.

Sanderson, C. (2004). *Seduction of Children: Empowering parents and teachers to protect children from child sexual abuse*. London: Jessica Kingsley Publishers.

Sanderson, C. (2013a). *Counselling Skills for Working with Trauma*. London: Jessica Kingsley Publishers.

Sanderson, C. (2013b). *The Spirit Within: A One in Four Handbook to Aid Recovery from Religious Sexual Abuse Across All Faiths*. London: One in Four.

Sanderson, C. (2015a) *Responding to Survivors of Child Sexual Abuse: A pocket guide for professionals, partners, families and friends*. London: One in Four.

Sanderson, C. (2015b) 'Analysis' in *Survivors' Voices: Breaking the silence on living with the impact of child sexual abuse in the family environment*. London: One in Four.

Sanderson, C. (2016). *The Warrior Within: A One in Four Handbook to Aid Recovery for Survivors of Childhood Sexual Abuse and Violence*, 3rd edition. London: One in Four.

Sanderson, C. (2019) *Numbing the Pain: A pocket guide for professionals supporting survivors of childhood sexual abuse and addiction*. London: One in Four.

Sanderson, C. (2022). *The Warrior Within: A One in Four Handbook to Aid Recovery for Survivors of Childhood Sexual Abuse and Violence*, 4th edition. London: One in Four.

Skovholt, T. M. & Trotter-Mathison, M. (2016). *The Resilient Practitioner: Burnout and Compassion Fatigue Prevention and Self-Care Strategies for the Helping Professions*. London: Routledge.

Smith, N., Dogaru, C. & Ellis, F. (2015). *Hear Me. Believe Me. Respect Me. A Survey of Adult Survivors of Child Sexual Abuse and their Experience of Support Services*. Ipswich: University of Suffolk.

van der Hart, O., Nijenhuis, E.R.S. & Steele, K. (2006). *The Haunted Self: Structural dissociation and the treatment of chronic traumatization*. New York: W.W. Norton.

van der Kolk, B. (2015). *The Body Keeps the Score: Mind, Brain and Body in the Transformation of Trauma*. New York, NY: Penguin Books.

Zaleski, K. L., Johnson, D. K. & Klein, J. T. (2016). Grounding Judith Herman's trauma theory within interpersonal neuroscience and evidence-based practice modalities for trauma treatment. *Smith College Studies in Social Work*, 86(4), 377–393.

Resources

Self-help books for survivors

Ainscough, C. & Toon, K. (1993, new edition 2000). *Breaking Free: Help for Survivors of Child Sexual Abuse.* London: Sheldon Press.

Bass, E. & Davis, L. (1990). *The Courage to Heal: A Guide for Women Survivors of Child Sexual Abuse.* London: Cedar.

Gil, E. (1983). *Outgrowing the Pain: A Book for and About Adults Abused as Children.* Rockville, MD: Launch.

Mines, S. (1996). *Sexual Abuse/Sacred Wound – Transforming Deep Trauma.* Barrytown, NY: Station Hill Press.

Parkes, P. (1989). *Rescuing the Inner Child: Therapy for Adults Sexually Abused as Children.* London: Souvenir Press.

Sanford, L. T. (1990). *Strong at the Broken Places: Overcoming the Trauma of Childhood Abuse*. London: Virago.

Wood, W. & Hatton, L. (1988). *Triumph over Darkness: Understanding and Healing the Trauma of Childhood Sexual Abuse*. Hillsboro, OR: Beyond Words Publishing.

For survivors abused by women

Elliot, M. (ed.) (1993). *Female Sexual Abuse of Children: The Ultimate Taboo*. Harlow: Longman.

For black women survivors

Wilson, M. (1993). *Crossing the Boundary: Black Women Survive Incest*. London: Virago.

For male survivors

Etherington, K. (1993). *Adult Male Survivors of Sexual Abuse*. London: Pitman Publishing.

Grubman-Black, S. D. (1990). *Broken Boys/Mending Men: Recovery from Childhood Sexual Abuse*. Blue Ridge Summit, PA: Tab Books.

Hunter, M. (1990). *Abused Boys: The Neglected Victims of Sexual Abuse*. New Britain, CT: Lexington.

Lew, M. (1988). *Victims No Longer: Men Recovering from Incest and Other Sexual Child Abuse*. New York, NY: Neuramount Publishers.

For survivors with learning disabilities

Hollins, S. & Sinason, V. (1992). *Bob Tells All*. London: St. George's Hospital Mental Health Library.

Hollins, S. & Sinason, V. (1992). *Jenny Speaks Out*. London: St. George's Hospital Mental Health Library.

Writings for survivors

Farthing, L., Malone, C. & Marce, L. (eds) (1996). *The Memory Bird: Survivors of Sexual Abuse*. London: Virago.

Autobiography

Angelou, M. (1983). *I Know Why the Caged Bird Sings*. London: Virago.

Chase, T. (1998). *When Rabbit Howls*. London: Sidgwick and Jackson.

Fraser, S. (1989). *My Father's House – A Memoir of Incest and of Healing*. London: Virago.

Smart, P. D. (2006). *Who's Afraid of the Teddy Bear's Picnic? A Story of Sexual Abuse and Recovery Through Psychotherapy*. London: Chipmunka Publishing.

Spring, J. (1987). *Cry Hard and Swim*. London: Virago.

Fiction

Walker, A. (1983). *The Colour Purple*. London: Women's Press.

For partners and families of survivors

Davis, L. (1991). *Allies in Healing: When the Person You Love was Sexually Abused as a Child*. New York, NY: Harper Perennial.

Graber, K. (1988). *Ghosts in the Bedroom: A Guide for Partners of Incest Survivors*. Deerfielf Beach, FL: Health Communication.

Messages from Parents whose Children have been Sexually Abused. Leeds: The Child and Family Resource Group, Leeds Community and Mental Health Trust.

From Discovery to Recovery: A Parent's Survival Guide to Child Sexual Abuse. Audio tape and booklet. Warwick: Warwickshire Social Services Department.

Help with relationships

Litvinoff, S. (1991). *The Relate Guide to Better Relationships*. London: Ebury Press.

Secunda, V. (1992). *When you and your Mother Can't be Friends*. London: Cedar.

For therapists

Hall, L. & Lloyd, S. (1989). *Surviving Child Sexual Abuse: A Handbook for Helping Women Challenge their Past*. Lewes: Falmer Press.

One in Four (2015). *Survivors' Voices: Breaking the silence on living with the impact of child sexual abuse in the family environment*. London: One in Four.

One in Four (2019). *Numbing the Pain: Survivors' voices of childhood sexual abuse and addiction*. London: One in Four.

Sanderson, C. (2004). *Seduction of Children: Empowering Parents and Teachers to Protect Children from Child Sexual Abuse*. London: Jessica Kingsley Publishers.

Sanderson, C. (2006). *Counselling Adult Survivors of Child Sexual Abuse*, 3rd edition. London: Jessica Kingsley Publishers.

Sanderson, C. (2010). *Introduction to Counselling Survivors of Interpersonal Trauma*. London: Jessica Kingsley Publishers.

Sanderson, C. (2011). *The Spirit Within: A One in Four Handbook to Aid Recovery from Religious Sexual Abuse Across All Faiths*. London: One in Four.

Sanderson, C. (2013). *Counselling Skills for Working with Trauma*. London: Jessica Kingsley Publishers.

Sanderson, C. (2013). *The Warrior Within: A One in Four Handbook to Aid Recovery from Childhood Sexual Abuse and Sexual Violence*, 3rd edition. London: One in Four.

Sanderson, C. (2015). *Counselling Skills for Working with Shame*. London: Jessica Kingsley Publishers.

Sanderson, C. (2015). *Responding to Survivors of Child Sexual Abuse: A Pocket Guide for Professionals, Partners, Families and Friends*. London: One in Four.

Sanderson, C. (2019). *Numbing the Pain: A Pocket Guide for Professionals Supporting Survivors of Childhood Sexual Abuse and Addiction*. London: One in Four.

van der Kolk, B. (2005). *The Body Keeps the Score*. London: Penguin Books.

Films featuring CSA

War Zone (1999)

A teenager uncovers a secret sexual relationship between his sister and father.

The Woodsman (2004)

A convicted child abuser must adjust to life after prison.

Capturing the Friedmans (2003)

The world of a seemingly typical, upper-middle-class Jewish family is ripped apart by allegations of child abuse.

Hard Candy (2005)

A young girl meets a photographer via the web. Suspecting he is a paedophile, she visits his home in an attempt to expose him.

London to Brighton (2006)

A crime-thriller genre playing on the idea of social realism with the themes of child prostitution and young runaways.

Beyond the Fire (2009)

A film about love and the effect of sexual abuse by a Catholic priest.

Precious (2009)

An adaptation of the 1996 novel *Push* by Sapphire.

Spotlight (2015)

A biographical drama about an investigation into Roman Catholic child sexual abuse in the Boston area.

Support services

One in Four

Advocacy service, counselling service (available over Skype and in several languages) and information for people who have experienced sexual abuse.

South London

219 Bromley Road, Bellingham, London SE6 2PG

Telephone 020 8697 2112

Email admin@oneinfour.org.uk

North London

8 Manor Gardens, London N7 6LA

Telephone 07580 733271

Email northlondon@oneinfour.org.uk

www.oneinfour.org.uk

Childline

Children can phone, send an online email, post on the Childline message boards or write to them for free if they are in trouble or are being abused. Childline can also help and advise parents, abusers and professionals.

Freephone helplines (24hr)

Children 0800 1111

Parents, abusers, professionals 0808 800 5000

Freepost NATN1111, London E1 6BR

Email via the website

www.childline.org.uk

Family Matters
Counselling service for children and adult survivors of sexual abuse and rape.

> 13 Wrotham Road, Gravesend, Kent DA11 0PA
> Telephone 01474 536661
> Helpline 01474 537392
> Email admin@familymattersuk.org
> www.familymattersuk.org

HAVOCA (Help for Adult Victims of Child Abuse)
Provides information to any adult who is suffering from past childhood abuse. Website includes survivors' forum.

> Email support friend@havoca.org
> www.havoca.org

Kidscape
Information about protecting children.

> Telephone 020 7730 3300
> www.kidscape.org.uk

Lifecentre
Telephone counselling for survivors of sexual abuse and those supporting survivors. Also offers face-to-face counselling and art therapy groups in West Sussex.

> PO Box 58, Chichester, West Sussex PO19 8UD
> Adult helpline 0844 847 7879
> Under 18s helpline 0808 802 0808
> Text 07717 989 022
> www.lifecentre.uk.com

National Association of People Abused in Childhood (NAPAC)

A UK charity providing support and information for people abused in childhood.

> CAN Mezzanine, 7–14 Great Dover Street, London SE1 4YR
> Freephone helpline 0808 801 0331
> Email info@napac.org.uk
> www.napac.org.uk

National Society for Prevention of Cruelty to Children (NSPCC)

A national UK charity helping children who have been abused to rebuild their lives, protecting those at risk and finding the best ways of preventing abuse from ever happening.

> Freephone helpline 0808 800 5000 (24hr)
> Freephone helpline (under 18s) 0800 1111 (24hr)
> Email help@nspcc.org.uk
> www.nspcc.org.uk

Positive Outcomes for Dissociative Survivors (PODS)

Helps people recover from childhood trauma and abuse, including CSA. Provides a service for both survivors and professionals working with them.

> 3 Archers Court, Huntingdon, Cambridgeshire PE29 6XG
> Telephone 01480 878409 (office)
> Support line 01480 413582
> Freephone helpline 0800 181 4420
> (Tuesday 6–8pm)
> Email info@pods-online.org.uk
> www.carolynspring.com

Rape and Sexual Abuse Support Centre (RASASC)

National helpline for female and male survivors, partners, friends and family.

> 24/7 rape and sexual abuse support line 0808 500 222
>
> Email info@rasasc.org.uk
>
> www.rasasc.org.uk

Survivors in Transition (SiT)

A support centre based in Suffolk offering counselling, information, advice, guidance and referrals to other specialist organizations for men and women who have experienced any form of CSA.

> Telephone 07765 052282
>
> Email info@survivorsintransition.co.uk
>
> www.survivorsintransition.co.uk

The Survivors Trust

A national umbrella agency for 130 specialist voluntary sector agencies that provide a range of counselling, therapeutic and support services.

> Unit 2, Eastlands Court Business Centre,
>
> St Peter's Road, Rugby, Warwickshire CV21 3QP
>
> Email info@thesurvivorstrust.org
>
> Telephone 01788 550554
>
> Helpline 08088 010808
>
> www.thesurvivorstrust.org

Websites

Resources

https://scottishattachmentinaction.org (Scottish Attachment in Action)
www.istss.org (International Society for Traumatic Stress Studies)
www.estss.org (European Society for Traumatic Stress Studies)
www.estd.org (European Society for Trauma and Dissociation)

www.isst-d.org (International Society for the Study of Trauma and Dissociation)
www.ukpts.co.uk (UK Psychological Trauma Society)
www.trauma-pages.com (David Baldwin's Trauma Information Pages)
www.understandingdissociation.com (Understanding Dissociation)
www.nctsn.org (National Child Traumatic Stress Network)
www.birthtraumaassociation.org.uk (Birth Trauma Association)
www.janinafisher.com (Janina Fisher's Trauma Pages)
www.familyrelationsinstitute.org (Family Relations Institute: Patricia Crittenden's Attachment Pages)
https://www.iasa-dmm.org (International Association for the Study of Attachment)

Young people's mental health
www.childmentalhealthcentre.org (The Centre for Child Mental Health)
www.childline.org.uk (Childline)
www.youngminds.org.uk (Young Minds)
www.headspace.com (Headspace)
www.smilingmind.com.au (Smiling Mind)
www.gires.org.uk (Gender Identity Research and Education Society)
www.mermaidsuk.org.uk (Mermaid)
www.switchboard.org.uk (Switchboard)

Index